INTERFAITH
HEROES

A Daily Reader of Inspirational Stories about
Leaders Reaching Out to Spiritually Unite People
and Build Stronger Communities

written and edited by

Daniel L. Buttry

Produced by Interfaith Partners of
The Michigan Roundtable for Diversity and
Inclusion

Read The Spirit Books

Find additional content and ongoing
discussion online at:

www.InterfaithHeroes.info

Photo credits:
We searched for original source information on all photos included
in this book. Most are identified as "public domain" by Wikimedia
Commons. In other cases, we sought permission. In the few cases
where credits were required we are including them here.

If we have used a photo in error, please contact us immediately at
admin@DavidCrummMedia.com or by mail at DCM-LLC, 42015
Ford Road, Suite 234, Canton, MI, 48187, and we will remove, revise
or add a credit to a future edition.

The photo of Muriel Lester is used with permission from the collections of International Fellowship of Reconciliation

The photo of Lanza Del Vasto is copyright © Community of the
Ark. Used with permission

The artwork of Fritz Eichenberg is copyright © Fritz Eichenberg
Trust, Licensed by VAGA, New York, NY. Used with permission.

The image of Satguru Sivaya Subramuniyaswami is courtesy of Hima-
layan Academy Publications.

The photo of Yogi Harbhajan Singh Khalsa is courtesy of SikhNet.

ISBN: 978-1-934879-00-9
1.0

Published by:
Read the Spirit Books
an imprint of
David Crumm Media, LLC
Canton, Michigan
www.ReadTheSpirit.com

Contents

Preface

For hundreds of years, Michigan has been moving the world – and the world has been moving to Michigan.

Thousands of years ago, tribes moved across North America and regarded Michigan's abundant waters as a highway designed for their livelihood by the Creator. For centuries, European traders, missionaries, scientists and writers followed, flocking to these same watery highways. By 1917, Henry Ford began building the largest integrated manufacturing plant on the planet here – The Rouge – to link raw materials shipped across our watery highways with the industry that would put the whole world on wheels and rename Detroit simply Motown.

Because of all that movement, Michigan has become a microcosm of the world's peoples. Here we already are living with the true cultural gift of the future: diversity.

Just as we were pioneers in movement – we are pioneers in resolving the greatest question of this new 21st Century: How shall we live together in our diversity?

That's why it is natural that religious leaders, community leaders, educators and journalists in Michigan are boldly launching in January 2008 a new national observance: The 1st Annual Interfaith Heroes Month.

This is who we are in Michigan.

This is our calling. We understand it and, at our best, we embrace it.

We've been working on this for a long time. A century ago, we were a prime destination in the Great Migration that transplanted entire African-American families from the South to the North, many of whom joined churches that funneled workers into Ford factories. This is a core chapter in American History – and eventually this Great Migration helped to integrate organized labor and American politics. African-American pioneers in blending faith, politics and social justice – giants like Paul Robeson, Malcolm X, Thurgood Marshall and the Rev. Dr. Martin Luther King Jr. – all walked the streets of Michigan during key periods of their lives.

Of course, Motown is as famous for its music as its motors. This also is a key chapter in American History. African-American artists summoned rhythms and rhymes from their rich spiritual heritage to fuel a creative flood that has reshaped the world from Aretha Franklin to Stevie Wonder with a galaxy of Motown stars spread out around them. As we prepare for the first Interfaith Heroes Month, that Motown legacy continues – as key artists with Motown roots helped to produce The Bible Experience, a best-selling audio Bible from the Michigan-based Zondervan publishing house. This enormous audio project was produced with theatrical flourishes that are proving so popular with consumers that this creative gift from

Michigan now is revolutionizing the whole concept of multimedia scriptures.

Think about this: These are just examples from one religious community.

We actually are a community of communities. That's true in all 50 states now. It's especially true in Michigan.

We're nearing the century mark in Michigan in innovative interfaith activism. In the 1920s, Reinhold Niebuhr, one of the most influential 20th Century theologians, shaped his social conscience on the gritty streets of Detroit. It was right here that he formulated material for his early best-seller: *Leaves from the Notebook of a Tamed Cynic*. He was a true Interfaith Hero on many occasions, including Detroit's city election day in 1925, when Niebuhr appeared at the top of the front page of the Detroit Free Press to plead with the city's voters not to elect a candidate with ties to the Ku Klux Klan. Niebuhr was joined by a rabbi and a priest that day in that front-page appeal to voters' consciences, co-sponsored by the Free Press.

That day became one of Michigan's founding milestones in the worldwide interfaith movement.

Of course, these forces are as explosive as they are inspiring. That sad truth is as obvious as the daily news.

Michigan also carries some of America's deepest spiritual scars.

Just as Niebuhr was restlessly pacing the city's streets, gleaning insights he would carry with him for the rest of his life – others were arising in Michigan as world-class foes to this idea. The infamous radio priest, the Rev. Charles Coughlin, has faded as a household name in this new century. But, he also is an essential part of American history. In the 1930s, before his broadcasts became so toxic that he finally was knocked off the airwaves, Coughlin's radio broadcasts were on par with the force of Oprah today. At his zenith, Coughlin received more weekly mail from across the U.S. than his nemesis in the White House: President Franklin D. Roosevelt.

We've all got such scars as Americans, don't we?

But here in Michigan, we've worked on soothing our collective scars more than most – which has become part of our unique gift to the world: our ability to reflect and to heal through celebrating religious diversity.

Our watchwords? Curiosity and respect.

Yes, Coughlin was a priest in the Catholic Archdiocese of Detroit. But, since that sad era, this Archdiocese has been in the vanguard of building innovative interfaith connections. Detroit Cardinal Adam Maida was among the first Catholic cardinals in the world to visit a mosque in the aftermath of the 9/11 attacks. The first ecumenical parochial school system in the U.S., Cornerstone Schools, was co-founded by Maida in Detroit.

Yes, Henry Ford's own sympathies with anti-Semitic voices in the 1920s and 1930s were deeply troubling. And, yes, Ford's voice was heard by countless Americans as part of an angry concert along with voices like Coughlin's broadcasts. These tragic viewpoints likely contributed to Americans slamming our doors on Jewish refugees trying to flee the rise of the Third Reich, historians say. Yes, it's a terrible wound.

And yet? In Michigan, the even more important history lesson that emerged was the healing that followed – decades of commitment by the Ford family and the Ford Motor Company to support religious, ethnic and cultural diversity. The Ford Interfaith Network, a visionary organization formed by Ford workers and executives in recent years, now is celebrated around the world as a model for integrating religious diversity into a secular workplace – and using that kind of recognition to build a stronger company.

That's what we've learned in Michigan. That's why we're pioneers. That's why we're the people called to make this bold declaration of a new national observance each January.

Now, this is very important: Like the pioneering Ford Interfaith Network, we are not trying to convert anyone to anything – except to the core American principle that we are stronger as a community when we all are free to express ourselves, including that deepest part of our lives: our faith.

It's certainly an American principle. We believe it should be a universal principle.

If you're seeking a place to come learn about these new directions in celebrating religious diversity, then come to Michigan. We're now home to: North America's largest Muslim center, the Islamic Center of America in Dearborn – and to one of America's oldest interfaith coalitions, pulled together from a host of groups.

Those are just two examples. There are so many more.

People around the world already have heard that we're the home state of Hamtramck, the little city made famous in headlines a few years ago when Americans learned that they could stand on its street corners and hear the welcoming peals of church bells mingling with the beckoning of muezzins calling Muslims to prayer – an inspiring chorus of sounds that's tragically endangered in other parts of the world.

We hear it here and celebrate it, now.

Or consider visiting with thousands of other people some of our many innovative centers and organizations:

» Focus:HOPE, the huge civil rights group and job-training center in Detroit that arose from the ashes of the 1967 civil rebellion.

» WISDOM, founded by Christian, Muslim and Jewish women who sponsor hands-on opportunities for women of all ages to build working relationships.

» Religious Diversity Journeys, organized by public-school educators to teach an appreciation of diversity to middle-school students.

» Reuniting the Children of Abraham, flexible workshops built around theatrical arts in which students teach adults about the importance of religious connections.

» Building Bridges Through Books, bringing Jews and Muslims together by sharing collections of books.

» Divine Light Media, an award-winning program that teaches high-school students to produce documentary films about religious diversity.

» The F5 Running Club, extending these ideas to athletes of all ages, abilities and faiths.

» The World Sabbath of Religious Reconciliation, an annual January event with a hopeful liturgy that's already spreading its observance around the globe.

» Interfaith Partners, a multi-faceted network of religious leaders, scholars and peace activists who are the creative force behind the collection of the 31 stories in this book.

» And, ReadTheSpirit, the new international network of media professionals who are reshaping the way religious voices are published, seen and heard around the world.

That's a lot, isn't it? Well, that's just the tip of Michigan's interfaith community. You'll find out more about our varied resources at the end of this book.

You may be able to find similar programs closer to your home – or to find out more about our pioneering efforts and grow your own new bridges based on these models. Our whole point here is to wake up readers around the world, through this annual observance, to the possibilities of such endeavors where you live, work and worship.

As the Founding Editor of ReadTheSpirit, I'm honored that our new Home Office is right here in Michigan. I'm also honored to work with the many partners who are declaring the start of this new annual observance, including the Michigan Roundtable for Diversity and Inclusion and its affiliated organization, Interfaith Partners.

But, wait: Have you heard this message clearly?

Do you realize that you're now a part of this, too?

Simply by opening up this book and starting to read – you're standing in a long line of men, women and young people – including the Rev. Dr. Martin Luther King Jr., whose birthday all Americans will celebrate this month. These Heroes reached out across religious boundaries to strengthen our global community. They're not alone. There are far more than 31 of these heroes around the world – and part of the lively creativity of this project is that we want you to help us nominate the 31 heroes we will honor in January 2009.

Go to <u>www.interfaithheroes.info</u> to learn more

about how you can do that.

Right now, you're already standing among the heroes. Feels good, doesn't it?

For centuries, Michigan has moved the world. Now, wherever you are at this moment, you've joined us in this journey.

Together, we're moving the world, again.

Happy Interfaith Heroes Month!

May you find the fuel to carry you across the new bridges that you surely will build with us!

David Crumm, writing from the ReadTheSpirit Home Office, December 2007

Author's Introduction

Each religious tradition honors a rich list of leaders who shaped its beliefs and practices. Many lived exemplary lives and are role models to this day. But, some of these religious leaders inspire us because they were peacemakers who dared to cross beyond their traditional boundaries to link with people from other faiths.

Some of these Interfaith Heroes are well known to us; others you'll learn about for the first time in these stories. Some were religious leaders; others were lay people whose faith shaped their lives in the secular world. Some were rulers and people of worldly power; others were ordinary people who exhibited their power through their extraordinary character.

In this 31-day collection of biographical sketches, you'll meet people who wound up deepening their own understanding of God and what it means to be human, because of the other spiritual perspectives they encountered.

Often, they took risks, working cooperatively with people of other faiths in the midst of fear and violence. Some even gave their lives to assist people from other religious communities.

Each of these heroes from the many religious traditions you will encounter in this book has something profound to teach us.

They continue to reach out across the centuries. Their lives pose a timeless question to us about whether our own faith divides or unites. Do we welcome diversity in the heroic tradition of the 31 people we will meet this month? Or do we fear it? Do we knit together lives? Or do we enable conflict?

There are many ways that this book can inspire, stimulate learning and encourage fresh commitments to building communities with interfaith partners. You can read these stories for personal reflection, asking yourself the questions for reflection at the end of each short biography. Or, you can use the book with a group from your place of worship or in an interfaith study or discussion group. Toward the end of this book, we'll offer more specific suggestions for study and action.

If you are a teacher in public or private schools, it may be possible to present some of these biographies as a diverse historical collection of figures who fall into the civil rights tradition of the Rev. Dr. Martin Luther King Jr. If you're reading this book along with men and women during Interfaith Heroes Month in January 2008, then King's well-known story will fall on his national holiday.

You are free to duplicate these stories in newsletters produced by your religious community, noting that the source is Interfaith Partners of the Michigan Roundtable for Diversity and Inclusion (MRDI). The 31 stories also will be published, day by day in January 2008, at www.InterfaithHeroes. info, along with personal responses to these stories by readers, plus an opportunity for you to share your own reflections – and news about public events that explore and celebrate diversity.

However you use this book, these examples of interfaith partnership stand as a heroic witness to peacemaking at a time of great violence in our history. Religiously fueled conflict rages in many parts of our world. The great question of the 21st Century is: How can we live with each other, when our backgrounds are so different? Will we learn from each other? Will we work together to shape a better world?

The "Next Steps" section at the end of this book provides some guidance for follow-up action with others in your community. Religion – and religious difference – is the leading issue as all of us around the world find our way into this new millennium.

May these 31 bright lights guide us.

May we be found worthy to be counted among them by the generations to come.

Daniel L. Buttry, writing in Michigan, Autumn 2007

Acknowledgements

This book grows from the journey of Interfaith Partners in Metropolitan Detroit.

Interfaith Partners is a non-partisan, grassroots network of faith communities dedicated to promoting the positive and healing role of religion in the life of our community and nation. We came together in the wake of the September 11, 2001 attacks with a commitment to inter-religious dialogue, education and cooperative service. We are Christians, Muslims, Jews, Hindus, Sikhs and people of other faiths who seek to learn from each other, to work alongside each other to build our shared community, and to be a witness together for respect being expressed to all faiths and all peoples.

Interfaith Partners has from its inception worked with the Michigan Roundtable for Diversity and Inclusion (MRDI), which earlier was called the Detroit chapter of the National Conference for Community and Justice. MRDI is a non-profit, human relations organization that seeks to eliminate discrimination and racism by working proactively across racial, religious, ethnic and cultural boundaries. The organization assists in building more inclusive communities, businesses and institutions through diversity training, advocacy, conflict resolution, interfaith collaboration, youth leadership training and community dialogue. MRDI has provided organizational support and staff for Interfaith Partners as part of its overall work of building a more justice community amid the diversity of the southeastern Michigan region.

In particular I would like to thank the Education Committee of Interfaith Partners for their work on this project. Bob Bruttell has provided editorial guidance, encouragement, ideas and writing. David Crumm helped in editing and writing the excellent "Questions for Reflection" at the end of each chapter. Sherri Schiff, Dan Appleyard, Barbara Talley, Gail Katz, Eide Alawan and Victor Begg provided suggestions and data for some of these heroes as well as editorial advice. Mas'ood Cajee, Ken Sehested, Victor Rembeth, Glen Stassen and Bill Gepford also provided excellent suggestions of heroes and directions for research. David Crumm and John Hile have welcomed the Interfaith Heroes project into their exiting web venture at www.ReadTheSpirit.com. With their involvement a synergy has developed that has expanded the horizons of the project in ways that will provided more interaction between people of various faiths across the country. The contributions of all these people have made the project far richer than initially conceived, illustrating the blessings that come to a diverse community of people willing to learn from each other and work together.

Daniel L. Buttry

chapter one

King Negus Ashama Ibn Abjar of Abyssinia (d. 630)

In the early 7th Century, King Negus Ashama ibn Abjar ruled the Kingdom of Axum, a land also known as Abyssinia, part of modern-day Ethiopia. "Negus" means "king" but also can serve as a proper name. This king is referred to in different sources both as Negus and as Ashama ibn Abjar. Many aspects of Axum's history remain mysterious to this day, because few records have survived, but this region of Ethiopia was among the first in the world to embrace Christianity.

Across the Red Sea from Abyssinia, a new religious tradition was unfolding in Arabia. Muhammad had begun receiving revelations and sharing them with a small group of followers. As people responded to Muhammad's teaching and began practicing this new faith, some of the pagan leaders in Mecca began to persecute Muhammad's followers. Muslims were mocked and assaulted, others had their businesses boycotted – and some were imprisoned in chains. Several Muslims died. Muhammad himself was protected by his uncle, but he told those who had no protection to flee for refuge to Abyssinia where he had heard of the famed mercy and equity shown by King Negus.

Late one night, the first eleven Muslims crossed over to Abyssinia. After they were given shelter by King Negus, 83 additional Muslim men and women fled for sanctuary. When the Meccans, also known as the Quraysh, found out about their flight from Arabia, they sent representatives to appeal to King Negus for their return, sweetening their appeal with gifts for him.

Though his advisers urged him to hand over the Muslims, King Negus called for all the parties to come before him to state their cases. Hadrat Ja'farradiya Allahu 'anhu, the spokesperson for the Muslim exiles, eloquently told the story of the refugees' lives. He described the sad conditions under which they lived before Muhammad began to preach among them. Then, he told about Muhammad's call for them to worship Allah and to live lives of prayer, integrity and justice. Finally, this spokesperson told about the tortures they had suffered from the Meccans and how they sought refuge.

When it was his turn, however, the Quraysh representative Amr ibn al 'As raised the issue of differences between the Muslims and Christians regarding the nature of Jesus. The Quraysh spokesman tried to use these differences to convince King Negus to ally with the Meccans in persecuting the Muslims.

But the king was a wise and fair man. Instead, he invited the Muslims to speak again. They responded by quoting from the Qur'an's extensive verses that describe Jesus and his birth by the Virgin Mary.

Then, Negus picked up a stick and said, "I swear, the difference between what we believe about Jesus, the Son of Mary, and what you have said is not greater than the width of this twig."

He refused to turn over the Muslim refugees and returned the gifts that the Meccans had hoped would sway his judgment. To this day, King Negus' action in the 7th Century is still a source of pride in both the Christian and Muslim communities in Ethiopia.

Questions for Reflection

• *Are we willing to provide refuge for people fleeing to our country even if their faith is different from ours?*

• *Do we focus more on the differences between us, and do we use those differences as a reason not to care for what they might suffer?*

• *Or, do we focus on the ways we are similar and regard the plight of others with mercy and kindness?*

Chapter two

Moses Maimonides
(1135-1204)

Moses Maimonides was the major medieval philosopher of the 12th Century. He was also a rabbi and the physician to the Grand Vizier Alfadhil and Sultan Saladin of Egypt. He was born in Spain during the golden age of Jewish culture in Cordoba.

However, when the Almohades, a radical Islamic sect, conquered Cordoba and threatened Jews who did not convert to Islam with death or exile, Maimonides fled from Spain along with many other Jewish men, women and children. Maimonides found refuge in more moderate Muslim communities, first in Morocco and eventually in Egypt. The Muslims of Cairo provided hospitality, and he lived and worked there the rest of his life.

Maimonides was one of the greatest Jewish thinkers ever, producing foundational philosophical works on Judaism. He wrote a commentary on the entire Mishnah, the ancient collection of Jewish texts that contains much of the faith's code for living. He wrote an enormously influential compilation of all of the more than 600 commandments for Jewish life contained in the Torah. He formulated 13 articles of faith, which still appear in most Jewish prayer books today.

Maimonides was also known for the breadth of his thinking and scholarship. He wrote medical works in Arabic, which have been translated into many languages and can still be found today. As a scholastic philosopher, he worked with the teachings of Aristotle as well as with Arab Muslim philosophers such as Ibn Rushd and Al-Ghazali.

Also, Maimonides worked diligently to reconcile scientific teachings with the teachings of his faith. In his mind, there could be no contradiction between what God revealed through the prophets and the findings of science and human reason. Maimonides' scholastic philosophy greatly influenced both Christian philosophers, such as Thomas Aquinas and Duns Scotus, as well as Arab Muslim philosophers who viewed him as one of their own.

Because Maimonides was open to diversity and was knowledgeable about many different streams of culture, his expertise enriched many traditions and faiths including his own. He wove together ancient Greco-Roman, medieval Arab, Jewish and Western cultures while retaining clear and cogent roots in his own Jewish faith.

Questions for Reflection

- *What do we know about the traditions and thinking within other cultures and faiths?*

- *Can you think of something helpful that you have picked up from a friend, neighbor or co-worker who is part of another tradition?*

- *Can we interact with those from different traditions in ways that enrich and refine our own religious thoughts and expressions?*

- *Do we recognize the differences among those in a religion who might treat people unjustly – and those adhering to that same religion who are merciful, just and provide sanctuary to those who need refuge?*

chapter three

Francis of Assisi (1181-1226) and Al-Malik Al-Kamil (1180-1238)

In the early 13th Century, amid the horrors of the Crusades, a Christian and a Muslim dared to cross the battle lines. The dialogue that took place surprised them both and provided a timeless model of risk-taking in pursuit of peace.

Francis of Assisi was born into a wealthy family and went off to war as a knight in the battles among Italy's city-states. Following a spiritual crisis, he made a radical break with his old life and committed himself to the spiritual renewal of the Roman Catholic Church. His spiritual discipline included simplicity, embracing poverty and seeing Christ in the poor. He founded a spiritual community based on these values, which became the Franciscan Order.

Francis held to radical nonviolence in an era when the Church was engaged in what was viewed as the "sacred violence" of the Crusades. Appalled by the brutality of the Crusades, Francis undertook a personal mission across the battle lines at Damietta to meet with the Muslim sultan, al-Malik al-Kamil. Francis sought to preach the gospel to the sultan, even if it meant his own martyrdom.

Instead of martyrdom, Francis received welcome and hospitality. Kamil was the nephew of the great military leader Saladin, who had defeated the European knights of the Third Crusade. Kamil was impressed by Francis' courage and sincerity and invited the monk to stay for a week of conversation. Francis was impressed by the devotion of the Muslims he met, including their call to prayer and use of prayer beads. Some scholars think that Francis brought these traditions back to Europe in the use of the Angelus and rosary. Neither converted the other, but both gained the respect of the other and learned from the other.

They parted as friends.

Francis returned after this encounter to try to persuade Cardinal Pelagius Galvani to make peace with the sultan, but to no avail. On the other hand, Sultan al-Kamil was ready for peace. After achieving victory, he provided humane treatment to the defeated Crusaders, which was in stark contrast to the atrocities committed by the Crusaders when they initially captured Damietta.

Al-Kamil eventually succeeded in making a peace agreement with Frederick II in 1229.

Questions for Reflection

- *Think of wars in the world today. Would you risk crossing into an enemy camp, hoping for hospitality? Can you think of anyone today who risks such wartime visits?*

- *Have you ever been pleasantly surprised by someone who you thought of as an enemy?*

- *Think of someone you regard as a foe. What steps would you take to arrange a conversation?*

chapter four

Jalal ad-Din Muhammad Rumi (1207-1273)

Jalal ad-Din Muhammad Rumi was a Persian Muslim poet and mystic theologian who lived in the 13ᵗʰ Century. He was born in Balkh, a Persian city in what is now part of Afghanistan. As a child, this region came under the threat of Mongol invaders. So, his family began a long trek that eventually ended with them settling in Konya in Asiatic Anatolia, now part of Turkey.

Throughout Rumi's life, there was a great deal of political and social conflict. Rumi's family was caught in a vise-like collision of forces, threatened by Mongol invaders from the East and Crusaders from the West.

Early in his adult life, Rumi was a prestigious

Islamic lawyer and scholar, but he developed a friendship with an eccentric mystic dervish named Shams-e-Tabrizi, which means Shams of Tabriz, a city in what is today Iran.

Shams introduced Rumi to the wondrous depths of mysticism and the two men became great friends, learning a great deal from each other. However, one night, Shams was murdered, allegedly by jealous followers of Rumi.

In his grief and his thankfulness for Shams' friendship, Rumi's creativity exploded in poetry that was stunning in its scope and creativity. Much of his poetry is famous for its ecstatic delight in ordinary encounters with nature and everyday activities. Rumi's poems in Persian are still widely read in Central Asia and the Middle East, and through translations, his work is very popular in the United States today. He also wrote poetry in Arabic, Greek and Oghuz Turkish.

Rumi explored themes and concepts that were central to Sufi thought, such as unity and turning toward the truth. He believed that music, poetry and dancing were pathways reaching toward God. After his death, Rumi's teachings led to the formation of the Mevlevi Order of "whirling dervishes," who created a sacred dance that represents a mystical journey through the mind and love to the "Perfect." Rumi taught that when one returns from this mystical journey, one will be able to love and serve the whole creation without prejudices that discriminate against a person's belief, race, class or nationality.

Early in his life, Rumi lived in a religiously diverse region. Balkh was rich with Buddhists, Muslims, Zoroastrians, Jews and Christians all living together. Rumi had friendly relationships with all the people he met in these various faith traditions. He was a devout Muslim, completing the hajj to Mecca early in his life. In a quote traditionally attributed to Rumi, the poet said, "I am not a Christian, a Jew, a Zoroastrian, or a Muslim." This quote was not an expression of unbelief. Instead, it reveals that Rumi believed deeply in humanity and in the oneness of God, which transcends human differences and touches all people.

In his personal life as well as his poetry, Rumi crossed lines of religious difference. His first wife was Muslim. After her death, Rumi married a woman believed to be a Christian, even though, at that time, Christian and Muslim warriors were entangled in the bloody battles of the Crusades. When he died, his funeral lasted 40 days, attended by grieving Muslims, Christians and Jews as well as by people from Greek, Arab and Persian cultures.

Rumi truly was a man whose heart and poetry embraced all humanity. Here are a few lines from his lengthy poem, "Masnavi," a cycle of verse that eventually stretched to more than 50,000 lines:

"Love's nationality is separate from all other religions,

The lover's religion and nationality is the Beloved (God).

The lover's cause is separate from all other causes

Love is the astrolabe of God's mysteries."

Questions for Reflection

- *Have you ever felt a passionate connection with people from another faith or culture?*

- *Have you ever mourned the loss of a person from a different background? Why did the death touch you so deeply?*

- *What spiritual poetry do you enjoy? Re-read or recite a passage that inspires you.*

chapter five

Jalaluddin Muhammad Akbar (1542-1605)

Jalaluddin Muhammad Akbar ruled the Mughal Empire in India from 1556 to 1605. He's more popularly known as Akbar the Great, because he was widely considered to be the greatest of the Mughal rulers. He expanded the Empire with key military victories against threatening neighbors. Akbar established greater internal stability through his long and steady reign. He also was a great patron of the arts, encouraging a flowering of Indian art and music.

Religious diversity and tolerance were hallmarks for Akbar's rule.

With a Hindu majority in India ruled by a Muslim elite, religious difference could have been very explosive. It had been in the past.

Instead, Akbar encouraged dialogue. He sponsored religious debates between Muslims, Sikhs, Hindus, Jains, Catholics and even atheists. He built the Ibadat Khana (House of Worship) as a place for such religious discussions. But, Akbar's policies went even further than this. To equalize religious opportunity in India, he abolished the pilgrim tax upon Jain holy places and the jizya tax on most non-Muslims (Hindu Brahmins and some Buddhists had been exempt). Some of his predecessors did not allow freedom of worship for Hindus and other religious groups, but Akbar reversed this policy.

But, he always pushed beyond these basic policies of balance to actively encourage a diversity of faiths. For instance, he preserved Hindu temples and established a positive relationship with the Roman Catholic Church. In addition, Akbar brought people of non-Muslim religions into his government.

In an age when royal multiple marriages were of great political import, Akbar married a Hindu woman, who became mother of the Mughal emperor Jahangir. He married other Hindu princesses, perhaps primarily for political reasons, but this nonetheless had an impact on the issue of religious tolerance. Akbar even married a Christian woman, and at least three of his grandsons were baptized as Catholics. Furthermore, his marital politics and relationship-building with the Hindu

Rajputs brought peace to an area that had been in turmoil under earlier Muslim rulers.

Akbar explored the teachings of the various religions so extensively that he ultimately tried to unify religious traditions into a new faith he called Din-i-Ilahi (Faith of the Divine), which drew from the traditions, beliefs and symbols of all the religions in India at that time. This proved to be an intriguing and ambitious failure. Only 18 people became official adherents of Din-i-Ilahi and the experiment fizzled out after Akbar's death.

However, learning from the teachings of others was important to Akbar – and his promotion of religious diversity made his country more peaceful, more stable and stronger as a nation.

Some accused him of being blasphemous, and a half-brother issued a fatwa, a ruling from Islamic law calling upon all Muslims to revolt. But Akbar was able to withstand these challenges and maintain his policies of tolerance for all religions.

His life was such an inspiring example that, reading about his life centuries later, the Poet Laureate of Great Britain Alfred Lord Tennyson, wrote a long poetic tribute to Akbar's vision, called "Akbar's Dream."

Questions for Reflection

- *Tennyson's poem is widely available online. You may want to read it yourself. In any case,* ask yourself this: Why is religious inspiration often linked to poetry? Have you ever written a poem yourself that expresses your views about religion?

• Akbar tried to create a religion that synthesized all the religions of his land. What do you see as critical elements of your spirituality that may be held in common with other faiths?

• What steps should we encourage to make religious tolerance and freedom a political reality for people who are not free today?

chapter six

Roger Williams (1603-1684)

Roger Williams founded the colony of Rhode Island in 1636 as a pure democracy, ruled by the majority but with the assurance that each person's religious conviction would be respected. Quakers, Baptists and Jews fled the restrictions of Massachusetts and England to come to Rhode Island and practice their faith freely. Native Americans were allowed to maintain their traditional religious practices. Williams formed the first Baptist church in American in Providence, though he later left the Baptists to become a "seeker."

This visionary early-American leader was born in England in 1603 and became a minister in the Church of England. He sailed to Boston in 1631. Williams quickly got in trouble with the religious authorities for his view that church and state should be separate. He argued for "soul liberty," his way of describing complete religious liberty for all. He joined the dissenting Pilgrims in Plymouth for two years, but his views were too broad for them. In 1635, the Massachusetts Bay Colony exiled Williams under pain of death for his religious convictions. Only the respect he had gained in large segments of the community saved him from hanging.

Williams fled south where he was befriended by the chiefs of the Narragansett tribe. Claiming that native peoples were the rightful owners of the land, rather than the King of England, Williams received a land grant land directly from the Narragansetts. There he founded Providence, Rhode Island. He learned the native languages, wrote a dictionary of the Algonquin language, and urged Europeans to enter into peaceful commerce rather than exterminating the native tribes.

He established Rhode Island as a settlement in which nobody would be turned away for their religious views or practices. In 1639, he helped to establish one of the first Baptist churches in America, which was organized around these same principles of a strict separation between church and state. Under Williams' guidance, Rhode Island was such a welcoming place that the second Jewish synagogue in America was established there.

His prophetic voice was far beyond the attitudes of his time. He argued against forced conversion of the Indians, comparing such acts to rape. With many conflicts developing between the European settlements and native peoples, Williams became a peacemaker, often mediating in disputes. During the King Philip's War he went unarmed to meet the warriors threatening to burn Providence. They refused his entreaties to spare the town, but they promised not to hurt him because he was an honest man. Today we regard the communities that were formed by Williams as models of American pluralism. However, in his day, his religious detractors called Rhode Island "the sewer of New England."

Roger Williams died in 1683 having established the first governmental body on this continent to constitutionally uphold religious liberty, a right which would later be enshrined in the Bill of Rights in the U.S. Constitution. He thought that the best protection for true religion was the freedom of all religious traditions – and even non-religion -- from interference by the state.

Questions for Reflection

* *Did you know about Williams already? Where did you learn about him? Recent history books are including more about Williams. Why do you think there may be a rising public interest in his story?*

* *What do you know about the religious*

traditions of native peoples that Williams so strongly defended? Talk with others about what you know about remaining native groups in your area.

- *Think of a person today who is standing up for the rights of religious minorities? How are their efforts going?*

- *What would you tell elected officials about the principles they should follow concerning religious freedom of expression? It's a complicated subject. What should be allowed? Should we change any of our laws concerning religious freedom? Why or why not?*

- *Do we see our own religious liberty tied to the religious liberty we extend to others? Why or why not?*

chapter seven

Moses Mendelssohn (1729-1786)

Moses Mendelssohn was an 18th-Century German-Jewish philosopher.

He was such a giant in the intellectual growth of European Jewish culture that some call him the third Moses (after Moses from the Bible and Moses Maimonides). Mendelssohn began his work in the fields of metaphysical philosophy and mathematics, engaging all the top scholars of his day with his elegant and lucid style of writing. He was hailed as a German Socrates.

Earlier in his academic career, Mendelssohn had been focused primarily on philosophy. A turning point in his intellectual passion came when Johann Lavater, a Christian admirer, challenged him to a debate, hoping to convert the Jewish philosopher. This exchange prompted Mendelssohn to delve deeper into his own Judaism. He translated the Pentateuch into German and wrote a commentary on Exodus. He also expanded beyond solely academic pursuits into ways that he could help emancipate Jews in Europe intellectually and legally.

His later writings dealt with the issues of religious emancipation and the relationship of church and state. In his book, *Jerusalem*, he held that the state has no right to interfere with the religion of its citizens, a call to reform that the philosopher Immanuel Kant found irrefutable.

In diverse societies he suggested the pragmatic principle of the possible plurality of truths. He argued that there may need to be different religions to deal with the diversity of humanity, and each one should be respected. For Mendelssohn, the true test of religion should be how it positively affects our human conduct.

Mendelssohn's own conduct was so noble and persuasive that the Christian philosopher and writer Gotthold Ephraim Lessing used him as the model for the title character in the 1779 play *Nathan the Wise*, which was an appeal for religious tolerance.

Mendelssohn also spoke out against the use of excommunication as a religious threat to people speaking their conscience. He personally worked on improving the relations between Jews and Christians, urging tolerance and a shared commitment to our common humanity.

Questions for Reflection

- *Can we engage in religious dialogue in such a way that we both go deeper into our own faith, yet deal respectfully with each other?*

- *What would happen if our faith was judged by the positive conduct of our lives?*

- *Mendelssohn's life sparked a new play. What plays, films or TV productions can you recall that model such positive spiritual values?*

chapter eight

Moses Montefiore
(1784-1885)

Sir Moses Haim Montefiore was the most famous British Jew in the 19th Century. He had an imposing physical presence, and his life spanned a full century. Business was his first career, working in a brokerage firm with his brother. He was elected Sheriff of London in 1837, and the next year he was knighted by Queen Victoria.

After he retired from his business at the age of 40, he became a lifelong philanthropist.

His first visit to the Holy Land in 1827 was a turning point in his life. He became a strictly observant Jew, and he became involved in advocacy for Jews suffering persecution or discrimination around the world. He journeyed to Turkey, Syria,

Italy, Russia, Morocco and Romania on highly publicized trips to represent Jewish communities in distress. Simply by visiting these communities, he brought the world's attention to the plight of the people. His advocacy for suffering Jews was strengthened by friendships he made with various world leaders, most notably Muhammad 'Ali Pasha, the Sultan of Egypt. Through his friendship with the Sultan, Montefiore secured the release of Damascus Jews who had been falsely accused of using Christian blood in religious rites, which was a notorious, centuries-old falsehood about Jews known as "blood libel."

Moses Montefiore's advocacy was not just for his own co-religionists. He raised funds for the relief of Christian refugees in Syria after thousands had been massacred by Druze militants. In Morocco while interceding for several Jews accused of murder, he also appealed for a Muslim who had been unjustly imprisoned for the murder of a Jew. He appealed to the sultan for fair treatment of all religious minorities.

As a philanthropist, Montefiore was active in many of the campaigns for reform in 19th-Century Britain. Often, he worked in alliance with other religious activists including evangelical Protestants. He helped organize the financial compensations to plantation owners to pave the way for abolishing slavery in the British Empire. His activist philanthropy was international in scope. Though he was primarily focused on the

poor Jewish communities, especially in the Holy
Land and around Jerusalem, in many of his relief
efforts he made equal donations to Jewish, Muslim
and Christian communities.

As one tribute on his 100th birthday said,
"Whenever the cry of distress reached your ears,
you opened wide the hand of relief without stint or
question, regarding the needy and the poor of all
sects and creeds as brethren."

Questions for Reflection

• *Does our generosity stop within our own
community of faith, or are we generous to
any who are in need?*

• *Talk with a friend about the human-rights
issues that most concern you, then ask:
Are we advocates for the rights of our own
community --- or are we advocates more
broadly for human rights?*

• *Think about a story you've heard in the news
in which someone from a minority group has
suffered. Is there anything, as an individual,
you can do to help relieve such suffering?
Montefiore actually traveled around the
world to help in such cases. We can't all do
that, but talk with a friend and ask: Is there
anything we can do as ordinary people to
relieve suffering and end injustices?*

chapter nine

Sarah and Angelina Grimké (1792-1873 and 1805-1879)

Sarah and Angelina Grimké were sisters born on a plantation in South Carolina. These belles of the South blazed a trail not only for abolitionists but for women's rights, and in so doing they blazed a trail for interfaith tolerance as well.

Sarah observed from an early age that slavery was a reprehensible institution, degrading slave and slave owner alike. She argued that slavery was not "Christian" and that slaves should be educated and freed. She traveled to Philadelphia where she met Quakers who encouraged her anti-slavery stance. When she returned to Charleston she began to speak out against slavery.

Her forceful abolitionist views were unacceptable to her home Episcopal Church. She felt drawn to the Society of Friends (Quakers) but discovered that, even to many Quakers, radical abolition was uncomfortable and that public advocacy of a cause by a woman was equally so. During a time when any participation in the religious practices of other faiths was grounds for excommunication, she determined to ally herself with people from other faiths who shared her abolitionist beliefs. Thus, religious toleration became a necessary part of her fight for the abolitionist cause. In her time and social context in the South, religious toleration was an issue concerned more with the diversity of Christian denominations than different religions.

As a child Angelina found slavery equally reprehensible. She objected to the law that slaves should not be taught to read. She taught her personal slave to read and, when caught, was severely reprimanded. Raised as an Episcopalian, she refused to be confirmed at age 13. Instead she joined the Presbyterian Church and began to take considerable interest in interfaith work. When her former minister tried to get her to renounce her new faith, she responded, "I could not conscientiously belong to any church which exalted itself above all others and excluded ministers of other denominations from its pulpit. ... I have lately succeeded in establishing a female prayer meeting among Baptists, Methodists, Congregationalists and Presbyterians."

When even the supposedly liberal Presbyterian Church did not support her abolitionist beliefs,

Angelina left the South and joined her older sister Sarah in Philadelphia. The Grimké sisters became celebrated agents of the abolitionist movement and were in high demand as public speakers. Their activism led to being banned from the Society of Friends, but they continued to press for complete abolition along with others from many faiths who shared their convictions.

They were among the first to make the argument that women's subjugation was tantamount to slavery in many ways. In 1838 in Boston, Massachusetts, Angelina Emily Grimké was the first woman to address an American legislature. Despite receiving many death threats they continued, at great risk to themselves, to advance the causes of interfaith tolerance, women's rights and abolition of slavery.

Questions for Reflection

- *Abolitionists with roots in Southern states faced threats and accusations of betrayal, but their most difficult step was seeing clearly that a common practice like slavery, practiced by people all around them, actually was wrong. Can you think of anything that's commonly accepted today, but that nevertheless might represent a dire moral evil?*

- *If you want to take on a social problem in your area, who could you contact from a different religious group to help you organize such an effort?*

- *The sisters' reflection on one moral evil, slavery, led them to see other evils as well, including sexism. Can you think of a moral problem that, if left unchecked, similarly leads to other serious ills? Are there patterns of social ills that feed into each other? If so, think of examples.*

chapter ten

Rabindranath Tagore (1861-1941)

Rabindranath Tagore was a literary giant in India. Born into a Bengali Brahmin family in Calcutta, Tagore founded an ashram in West Bengal that included an experimental school. He believed that God was found through personal purity and service to others. Tagore was known primarily for his poetry which was deeply influenced by the mysticism of the Hindu Upanishads but at the same time was accessible to many Western readers. In 1913 he was awarded the Nobel Prize for Literature becoming Asia's first Nobel laureate.

However, Tagore was prolific in many other artistic fields. Besides his poetry, Tagore produced many novels, short stories and dramas. He wrote non-fiction works on diverse topics: Indian history, linguistics, travelogues and science. He composed more than 2,000 songs, including many devotional hymns and the national anthems for both India and Bangladesh. When he was sixty he began to draw and paint, and his art was exhibited in Paris and London.

Tagore was a controversial figure in Indian politics. He supported the Indian independence movement and was a friend of Gandhi, but he also disagreed with Gandhi over many issues. He was especially virulent in his attacks on nationalism. He denounced fascists, Japanese and American nationalists, and even the nationalism in the Indian independence movement.

He spoke out against India's "abnormal caste consciousness," decrying the evils of social systems in India that left millions in poverty and labeled entire groups of people as "untouchable." He raised feminist concerns in his writings, calling for liberation of women from many of the customs in marriage. In his stories, he attacked those who still glorified the custom of self-immolation by women after their husbands' deaths.

Tagore's writings were influenced by many religious streams. The Muslim mystical poet Hafez was an inspiration to him. He used a Buddhist story of Ananda, one of Gautama Buddha's disciples, who asked an untouchable girl for water, as an exemplary tale for his Hindu culture. During Tagore's travels he engaged with many people in discussions of a transcendent humanism. He addressed the annual Quaker gathering in London, and became a friend and associate of Charles Andrews, the Christian missionary who was Gandhi's protégé. Tagore was deeply disturbed by the tensions and violence between the Hindu and Muslim communities in India. He explored these issues in his writings, taking on the religious zeal that leads to bigotry and violence, especially when wedded to nationalism.

Questions for Reflection

- *Think of another author or artist who draws from more than one culture and faith. There have been many of them from William Shakespeare's era to today. Is there one you enjoy? Why do you like reading or seeing these expressions of other cultures?*

- *Many TV programs and films now explore these connections as well. Is there one you enjoy? Talk with a friend and share your favorites.*

- *Do you agree with Tagore that nationalism can be a threat to our basic religious values? Why might that be a problem?*

chapter eleven

Henrietta Szold (1860-1945)

Henrietta Szold was born in 1860, one of eight daughters of a Baltimore rabbi and his wife. She became a passionate student of Judaism, and was even allowed to study at the Jewish Theological Seminary, only open to men at that time. She became an early Jewish voice for women's rights.

Szold founded Hadassah Women, the largest Jewish organization in the U.S. As a Zionist organization Hadassah was involved in the 1930s in saving Jewish youth from Germany and then later from across Europe. About 22,000 Jewish children and youth were rescued from the Nazis through Hadassah's work, a legacy built upon the foundation of Szold's advocacy and activism.

From Hadassah's inception, Szold opposed

discrimination and she voiced this important value in a prophetic way. This became a complex issue as Hadassah began to engage in healthcare in Palestine.

During and following World War I, American Jews organized the American Zionist Medical Unit to deal with some of the suffering of Jews in Palestine. The huge problems and organizational chaos led Szold to come to Palestine in 1920 to take over the organization. She established the Hadassah Medical Organization to care for women and children. She insisted that the organization work with Arabs, Muslim and Christian, as well as Jews, providing the same care to all people with the best medical technology possible.

Following her model, the organization served people of all origins and religions equally and cooperatively. The Hadassah Hospital in Jerusalem, which grew out of the original organization that Szold headed, is now the premier medical institution in Israel and the entire Middle East.

Szold envisioned nondiscriminatory health care as providing a bond between Jews and Arabs for building common community – but this has not been easy amid the volatile politics and frequent violence in the region. In 1948, before the state of Israel was established, 77 Jewish doctors and nurses from the hospital were killed by Arab soldiers.

Nevertheless, Hadassah has continued to practice cooperation, coexistence and nondiscrimination even as Hadassah treats more victims of on-going violence than any other medical center. Szold's work has continued beyond her death through the staff of Hadassah, resulting in a nomination of the Hadassah Medical Organization for the Nobel Peace Prize in 2005.

Through the most difficult times, the cooperative context of Hadassah's healthcare has provided opportunities for creating bridges of communication and initiatives for peace.

Questions for Reflection

- *Are you aware that religious communities historically were the innovators in organizing hospitals? In your region, what religious groups share in providing healthcare?*

- *Have you ever met a hospital chaplain? If you're part of a discussion group, inviting a local chaplain to speak is one way of learning more about cooperation between faiths.*

- *Access to healthcare is a concern shared across religious boundaries these days. What do you know about the situation in your area? Do people have trouble finding healthcare? Volunteering in programs related to healthcare is a great way to quickly find yourself working closely with people of other faiths.*

chapter twelve

Mohandas "Mahatma" Gandhi (1869-1948)

Mohandas K. Gandhi led the movement in India for independence from British colonial rule. His approach to nonviolence was called satyagraha, with literally means "truth—hold on" and has been popularized as "truth force." He initially developed his nonviolent philosophy and practice during the twenty years he lived in South Africa. Trained as a lawyer, he led Indians in South Africa in protests against the racist policies of the white government, culminating in 1914 with some concessions, granting new rights for the Indian immigrant community.

Returning to India, Gandhi, now given the honorific title "Mahatma," threw himself into the struggle against British colonialism. He organized campaigns of non-cooperation with British political and economic power, highlighted by his "Salt March" across India to the sea where he made salt in defiance of the British monopoly on this vital commodity. Eventually, through a long, complex struggle India achieved independence in 1947.

Gandhi also struggled for justice within Hindu society, especially calling for raising the status of the "untouchables." Though he was from an upper caste, he advocated an end to the social and economic injustices in the caste system. His conviction on this matter was so intense that he launched a "fast to the death" from prison in one campaign that successfully eased a particular restriction.

Gandhi was a devout Hindu, but he drew much of his inspiration from the teaching of Jesus and the Russian Christian pacifist Leo Tolstoy. Many Christian friends lived in his ashram and joined him in his actions. Gandhi often quoted the Christian scriptures and said to his Christian friends, "to be a good Hindu also meant that I would be a good Christian. There was no need for me to join your creed to be a believer in the beauty of the teachings of Jesus or try to follow His example." The three books he carried with him everywhere were the Bhagavad Gita, the Bible and the Quran.

Gandhi also bridged the two largest religious groups in India: Hindus and Muslims. He worked closely with Abdul Ghaffar Khan, a Muslim friend and nonviolent activist for independence. They each took the principles of their own faiths and applied them to the same nonviolent practices in the same struggle for freedom.

When violent riots erupted in India between Hindus and Muslims, Gandhi pleaded for peace. To underscore his message, he began long fasts directed to his own Hindu community, calling upon them to halt the violence. Following the successful end of inter-communal violence in Calcutta in response to his fast, Gandhi was assassinated in 1948 by a Hindu extremist.

Questions for Reflection

- *Have you risked yourself in any way to help people who are marginalized or threatened because they are part of a minority group? If you feel moved to do so, how could you take such a step?*

- *Have you read the three scriptures Gandhi always carried? Copies are easily available in stores or online. Consider reading a new scripture with a friend and talking about what you find in the text. How is the new text different from your own?*

- *Is fasting a part of your religious tradition? It's a custom found in most faiths. If you haven't done so already, try fasting – even from a single meal – and use the time to reflect on* other people in the way Gandhi did as he fasted.

chapter thirteen

Abdul Ghaffar Khan
(1890-1988)

Abdul Ghaffar Khan was a Pashtun born under the British occupation of the Indian sub-continent. In the North-West Frontier Province (now part of Pakistan) the Pashtuns were noted for fierce blood feuds and for their staunch resistance to the British. In turn, the British were known for responding in equally brutal fashion.

Ghaffar Khan joined the movement for independence and was moved by the calm, strong demeanor of the Hindu Mahatma Gandhi. He forged an Islamic teaching of nonviolence based on the Muslim values of amal (selfless service), yakeen (faith) and muhabat (love). Through his leadership as a teacher and organizer, he developed a nonviolent army called the Khudai Khidmatgars (Servants of God) to resist the British. Over 100,000 Pashtuns joined this red-shirted army who swore an oath to live a simple life of service, refraining from violence or any form of revenge. Ghaffar Khan spoke of this form of struggle as a jihad conducted with only the enemy holding swords.

Ghaffar Khan's Khudai Khidmatgars became one of the most potent forces for protest against British colonial rule through protests and strikes. In the city of Peshawar, British soldiers fired on the Khudai Khidmatgars, killing hundreds and wounding over a thousand, though the protesters were unarmed. As people fell, new ranks of the "red shirts" would boldly step forward to nonviolently risk being shot. One unit of British soldiers were so moved by their nonviolent courage that they refused to follow orders en masse. It was later said that the British feared a nonviolent Pashtun more than a violent one, because their nonviolent resistance made the North-West Frontier Province ungovernable.

Gandhi and Ghaffar Khan worked alongside each other toward a vision of an India in which Hindus and Muslims could live in peace. They learned from each other, respected each other's faith and were influenced by each other. Ironically, they would both suffer from their own co-religionists because of their prophetic call for a multi-religious nation. Gandhi was killed by a Hindu extremist for urging peace with Muslims, and Ghaffar Khan was imprisoned by an Islamic government in Pakistan for being "pro-Indian."

After the break-up of India into India and Pakistan, Ghaffar Khan tried to obtain democracy for his Pashtun people in both Afghanistan and Pakistan, maintaining nonviolent convictions and actions. He spent over 30 years in prison for his convictions.

He died in 1988 at age of 98 under house arrest, a life-long witness for the compatibility of nonviolence and Islam. He was nominated for the Nobel Peace Prize. He once said, "My religion is truth, love and service to God and humanity. Every religion that has come into the world has brought the message of love and brotherhood. Those who are indifferent to the welfare of their fellowmen, whose hearts are empty of love, they do not know the meaning of religion."

Questions for Reflection

- *Have you ever alienated someone from your own community by building a bridge to a different community?*

- *Imagine Ghaffar Khan under house arrest. Many influential peace activists have suffered this fate. What could you do within your own home to spread a message of religious and cultural tolerance?*

- *"Prisoner of conscience" is a phrase often used for people in these situations. Can you find a way to peacefully support such prisoners, especially those who may come from an entirely different culture than your own?*

chapter fourteen

Muriel Lester (1885-1968)

Muriel Lester was born into a wealthy Baptist family in England in the late-1800s. Early in her life she showed a non-conformist radicalism in her faith, especially over concerns for social justice. While traveling by train through the slums of London she began to see poverty as a moral challenge. She committed herself to voluntary poverty, moved into the Bow neighborhood of London and began to help poor families as a social worker. She purchased an old church building and turned it into Kingsley Hall, a social service center. Lester mobilized people in the community to determine together what issues to address and how to deal with them. She was able to empower people, especially those who thought they had no power.

During World War I, Lester became a pacifist and joined the newly formed International Fellowship of Reconciliation (IFOR). Her post-war efforts at famine relief launched the movement that became the Save the Children Fund. Through her IFOR connections, she invited the son-in-law of Rabindranath Tagore, the great Hindu poet and philosopher, to speak at Kingsley Hall. In turn, he invited Lester to India.

On that visit, she developed a life-long friendship with Gandhi. Gandhi challenged her, "Speak the truth, without fear or exaggeration, and see everyone whose work is relative to your purpose. You are on God's work, so you need not fear men's scorn." When Gandhi came to Britain in 1931 he stayed at Kingsley Hall for three months. As a Christian and as a Hindu, Lester and Gandhi took the teachings of Jesus and applied them to the struggles for freedom from colonial power in India.

In 1933 Lester turned the leadership of Kingsley Hall over to her sister. Lester then became the traveling secretary for IFOR. She conducted prayer schools around the world with people of many different religions: Muslims, Jews and Hindus. Wherever she found violence and injustice, she worked to mobilize people of faith to struggle against those problems.

Muriel Lester lived the message of reconciliation in every sphere of human life, including religious reconciliation. In her own words, she sought to share "the vision of God as Love and Beauty, and the sense of comradeship which brings strength and vigour to the weakest."

Questions for Reflection

- *What does this phrase, "the vision of God as Love and Beauty," mean to you? How might it relate to peace and justice?*

- *Why do you think Gandhi said that "exaggeration" was as great a danger as "fear" when people speak out in public?*

- *How do you express hospitality in your home, school, house of worship or place of work for people who are of a different faith or culture?*

chapter fifteen

Etty Hillesum (1914-1943)

Etty Hillesum was a young Jewish woman from Amsterdam who was swept up by the Nazi occupation and Holocaust. She died in Auschwitz on November 30, 1943, at the age of twenty-nine, but she is known for the vitality of her witness for life and love amid the horrors of hatred and destruction.

For the last two years of her life, she kept a diary that was discovered and published forty years after her death. Now, the lives of people from many faiths have been shaped by Hillesum's deep spirituality. In her diary, she expressed her mystical relationship with God that enabled her to live fully and with moral clarity in the face of great suffering.

She worked as a typist for the Jewish Council

in Amsterdam, a privilege that kept her from being deported for awhile. But then she volunteered to accompany her fellow Jews to the camps, feeling a spiritual calling to be present at the heart of the suffering, to "become the thinking heart of the concentration camp." She believed the effort to preserve in one's heart the spirit of love and forgiveness was the greatest task one could take up. She did not glorify suffering as such, but she desired to redeem the experiences of suffering by finding God deep within. Even in the concentration camps with death ever present she envisioned the way she lived her life as a way to prepare for a new age whether or not she would survive to see it.

Though clearly rooted in her Jewish faith and scriptures, she drew upon a wide range of writers for her own reflection and spiritual development, including Rilke, Augustine, and Dostoevsky. When criticized for talking about love of enemies and sounding too much like she was expressing Christianity, she responded, "Yes, Christianity, why ever not?"

She did not participate in organized religion, but she held strongly to a personal encounter with God that could be discovered both at the depths of one's own being and in other people as well.

Questions for Reflection

- How could you become "the thinking heart"

for the people you will encounter in your life today?

• How can we maintain our spiritual balance and clarity in the face of great suffering? When things get tough, are we tempted to get angry with other people and even begin to see other people in distorted ways?

• Have you ever kept a journal or diary? Consider jotting down your reflections on a regular basis and see what begins to flow in your writing.

chapter sixteen

Albanian Muslims During the Holocaust

For many years the heavy curtain of Communism shrouded Albania from the view of the rest of the world. When that curtain was lifted in 1991 amazing stories emerged about the role of Albanian Muslims saving Jews during the Holocaust that swept across Nazi-occupied Europe.

When the German Nazi army occupied Albania it wasn't long before the Albanians were ordered to surrender their Jewish citizenship. That prompted a massive movement among Albanians from top officials to grassroots villagers to shelter Jews. Most of those engaged in the movement were Muslims. Hospitality is a deeply held value for Albanians, so they went to great lengths and took personal risks to shield the Jews from the Nazis. Non-Jewish Albanians would steal identity cards from police stations for Jews to use. The Albanian underground threatened to execute anyone who turned a Jew in to the Nazis. Jews from Serbia, Austria and Greece found refuge in Albania.

As astonishing as this may sound: Not a single Jew from Albania ended up in the concentration camps.

Dr. Anna Kohen, speaking at a Holocaust remembrance in New York City told about her family fleeing to a mountain village. They all took Muslim names. She said, "Everyone in the village knew they were Jews, but not one person betrayed them." Her family's story was repeated again and again throughout Albania. Sulo Mecaj, a farmer from the village of Kruja who sheltered 10 Jews in his attic, was asked what would happen if the Nazis burned down his house with the Jews inside. "My son will go into the attic with the Jews and suffer their fate." At the end of World War II there were more Jews living in Albania than at the start of the war, the only country in Europe where this happened.

Faith as well as culture played a major role in this life-and-death hospitality. Shyqyri Myrto helped Josef Jakoel and his sister Eriketa evade Germans going house to house searching for them. He said, "Our Muslim religion says we must help someone who is in danger in difficult times."

His friend Bequi Qogja said, "We all have one God, and he has commanded us to help others. It's the same thing Jesus said, that Muhammad has commanded, and actually your Moses said the same thing."

Albanian protectors of the Jews were named in

the "Rescuer's Wall" at the U.S. Holocaust Museum in 1995. Albanian Muslim names are inscribed at the Yad Vashem Holocaust Memorial in Jerusalem with the "Righteous Among the Nations."

Questions for Reflection

- *Don't you feel an almost electric jolt of inspiration reading this story? In the teeth of deadly, overwhelming, military might – not a single Jew was taken from Albania. Ponder this truth. Today, can you summon a little more bravery to help another person?*

- *In Josef's story, why would his son feel moved to perish with the people his family had hospitably protected? Have you ever experienced a code of hospitality so all encompassing?*

- *In your community, what minority groups needs the protection of neighbors?*

chapter seventeen

Martin Buber (1878-1965)

Martin Buber was a Jewish philosopher and theologian who had a profound impact on both Jewish and Christian thinking. He embodied the ideal of dialogue and understanding between people of different faiths and even conflicting interests. He felt that faith could play a positive role in creating a more humane world.

He was born in Vienna, Austria in 1878. As a student, Buber strayed from his religious roots, but the anti-Semitism in Europe prompted him to join the early Zionist movement. As he went through a religious reawakening, he extensively studied Hasidism, the Jewish renewal movement. Though he never became Hasidic, he embraced their call to holiness in everyday life. He called for people to affirm the world for God's sake so that we could transform it.

As professor of Jewish religious history at the University of Frankfurt, Buber published his classic book, *I and Thou*, about the relational nature of human existence. He held that the quality of our relationships should be the basic measure of the quality of our humanity.

When the Nazis came to power, Buber was promptly dismissed from his academic position and he began to campaign for Jewish rights against the rising tide of fascism. By 1938, he was so restricted by the Nazis that he decided to escape from Germany to Jerusalem where he became a professor at Hebrew University.

Buber retained his Zionism, but he felt that nationalist expressions were headed in the wrong direction. He called for a "Hebrew Humanism" in which Jews and Palestinian Arabs could find a just and cooperative arrangement to deal with issues of the land. The outbreak of war in 1948 left him deeply saddened, but still committed to building human relationships.

Buber had a major impact on Christian thinking through his popularization of Jewish spirituality and mysticism. He recognized the Jewishness of Jesus and saw him as an example of some of the highest ideals in Judaism. However, he saw that there were many irreconcilable differences between the two faiths, yet these differences should not stop dialogue.

He wrote, "Whenever we both, Christian and Jew, care more for God Himself than for our images of God, we are united in the feeling that our Father's house is differently constructed than our human models take it to be." Martin Buber died in Jerusalem in 1965.

Questions for Reflection

- *How do we measure "the quality of our humanity"? Do we do it through "the quality of our relationships" like Buber – or in other ways?*

- *What do you think of Buber's idea that "our images of God" sometimes get in the way of "God?" Can you think of problematic images of God?*

- *Are you able to see the irreconcilable differences between two faiths – and still talk constructively with someone from another faith?*

chapter eighteen

André Trocmé (1901-1971)

André Trocmé was the Protestant pastor of the small village of Le Chambon in France. Born into a Huguenot family in Catholic France he understood first-hand the experience of living in a religious minority. Then, in World War I, he was a refugee as his family fled the horrors of the trenches. Perhaps these experiences helped shape his compassion toward those who were vulnerable and homeless.

When he took the pastorate at Le Chambon in 1934, Trocmé preached on the principles of love of God and one's neighbor, based on Jesus' teachings in the Sermon on the Mount. Those principles, lived out by Trocmé and Magda, his wife, filtered into the congregation. Then in 1940 France fell to

Nazi Germany. Le Chambon was in the formally independent Vichy region, but as fascism spread into the countryside Trocmé spoke against the rising spirit of fear and hatred. As the stand of the village against fascism was passed on by word of mouth, refugees and those fearing persecution made their way to Le Chambon.

In 1942 the Nazis ordered all Jews to be delivered for deportation. Formal resistence to the deportation began around the church elders and presbytery. Jewish refugees were hidden in the village and surrounding homes in spite of searches by the Vichy police and later the Gestapo. Trocmé was arrested briefly and later went into hiding himself, but the resistance continued.

Approximately 2,500 Jews were sheltered by the villagers of Le Chambon, a small number amid the slaughter of millions in the Holocaust. But, in the entire nation of France, Le Chambon was the safest place for Jews to be. As the preacher and conscience of his community, André Trocmé called his flock to a faith that was willing to risk one's own life to protect the lives of those victimized by hatred and bigotry.

André Trocmé died in 1971. In the following year Israel posthumously awarded him the Medal of Righteousness. A tree was planted in the Yad Vashem memorial, honoring him as one of the "righteous among the nations."

Questions for Reflection

- *Trocmé and his followers saw a rising tide of fear and bigotry in fascism and the looming Holocaust. Are there any destructive tides you see rising today?*

- *Have you ever sheltered someone? When a relative was disabled or lost a job? During a natural disaster? Would you shelter someone in your home from a different faith and culture?*

- *What could you do – in talking with friends, neighbors and others in your community as Trocmé once did – to warm them to the idea of helping people who seem to be quite different than the rest of us? What values from your faith would be most helpful in developing such an open hospitality?*

chapter nineteen

Howard Thurman
(1900-1981)

Howard Thurman was an author, philosopher, theologian, pastor, educator and civil rights leader. The grandson of a slave, he graduated from Morehouse College as valedictorian in 1923. Shortly thereafter he was ordained as a Baptist minister, but his studies with the Quaker mystic Rufus Jones introduced him to a broader range of spirituality. Thurman became the Dean of Rankin Chapel at Howard University.

While leading a student "Pilgrimage of Friendship" trip to India, Thurman and his wife, the former Sue Bailey, had a meeting with Mahatma Gandhi that gave focus to a growing passion in his ministry. He envisioned an interracial church in the days when most blacks were excluded from white churches. When Thurman asked, "What is the greatest enemy that Jesus Christ has in India?" Gandhi responded, "Christianity." Thurman resolved to remain within his Christian tradition but work at overcoming the divisive influences within race and religion that split so much of society.

By 1944, Thurman had joined with a small interracial circle of friends, initially Quakers and Episcopalians, to found a neighborhood church in San Francisco called The Church for the Fellowship of All People, the first intentionally interfaith congregation in the United States. Thurman was chosen as founding co-pastor along with Dr. Alfred Fisk. They sought to preach truths that would be embraced by all people of faith and offer expressions of spirituality from many global cultures and religions. Jews, Buddhists and Hindus joined in the church as well as people who were alienated from all organized religion. Thurman's basic theme was, "We are one at any level."

Speaking of his work in promoting inter-religious fellowship, Thurman said: "Man builds his little shelter, he raises his little wall, builds his little altar, worships his little God, organized the resources of his little life to defend his little barrier, and he can't do it! What we are committed to here, and what many other people in other places are committed to, is very simple – that it is possible to develop a religious fellowship that is creative in character and so convincing in quality that it inspires the mind to multiply experiences of unity – which experiences of unity become over and over and over again more compelling than the concepts, the ways of life, the seeds and the creeds that separate men. We believe that in the presence of God with His dream of order there is neither male nor female, white nor black, Gentile nor Jew, Protestant nor Catholic, Hindu, Buddhist, nor Moslem, but a human spirit stripped to the literal substance of itself."

In 1954 Thurman left to become the first black Dean of Marsh Chapel at Boston University. He was an active voice in the civil rights movement, exerting a major influence on the spirituality of the young Martin Luther King, Jr. Following his death in 1981, Howard Thurman's writings continue to speak about spirituality and justice, influencing the vision and work of new generations.

Questions for Reflection

- *Gandhi's words to Thurman are powerful and could be applied to all of the world's faiths in at least some eras and situations. What elements of our faith sometimes are used to divide people rather than to unite communities?*

- *Would you feel comfortable in joining an interfaith church? How could such a church be organized today that would appeal to you?*

- *What do you think of Thurman's charge that many people worship "little" gods? If you agree with him, then describe some things that can keep a person's concept of God too small. How "big" can your vision of God become?*

chapter twenty

Lanza del Vasto (1901-1981)

Lanza del Vasto was born to a noble family in Italy in 1901. After studying philosophy he journeyed to India in 1936 where he studied under various Hindu holy men. He met Mahatma Gandhi and lived at Gandhi's ashram long enough to become deeply acquainted with his philosophy of nonviolence and its practice. Gandhi gave him the name Shantidas, "Servant of Peace."

Shantidas returned to Europe committed to the work of reconciliation among religions and resistance to violence in all its forms. He and his wife Chanterelle founded the Community of the Ark in France in 1948 as a community of common prayer to apply nonviolence in every area of life. They sought to be as self-sufficient as possible. From the base of their community they launched protests against exploitation and violence. They worked on campaigns against concentration camps, against torture during the Algerian war, and for the rights of conscientious objectors.

Del Vasto was a committed Catholic, and he worked tirelessly to remind the Catholic Church about the gospel message of peace. He fasted for forty days in Rome as part of an appeal to the Pope to issue a statement against the arms race. In recognition of his witness he was given an advance copy of Pope John XXIII's "Pacem in Terris". This Servant of Peace died in 1981.

The Community of the Ark was open to people of all religious faiths. Del Vasto maintained his own spiritual roots in Catholicism, but he was able to learn from people in other religious traditions, recognize and embrace what was held in common, and work together on issues of conscience and human rights. He held up to the whole world a hopeful vision of a future in which nonviolence would triumph in human relations.

Until his death, he was known around the world as a person of peace, strength and joy.

Questions for Reflection

- *Here is another interfaith hero who used fasting as a powerful spiritual discipline in an effort to reshape the world. Millions of people around the world fast. Have you tried it? If you have, has your fasting focused solely on interior reflection? Have you tried fasting to have a personal impact on the larger world?*

* *If you set out to explore and learn from another faith, as del Vasto did, where would you start? Which faith, beyond your own, intrigues you?*

* *If you welcomed a visitor from another faith, what are the aspects of your own faith that you would want to share first?*

chapter twenty-one

The Rev. Dr. Martin Luther King, Jr. (1929-1968)

The Rev. Dr. Martin Luther King, Jr., was a Baptist pastor who ultimately gave up his own life to change life for all Americans. His powerful, poetic appeals called upon us all to act in new ways on our deeply held sense of justice. His impact was so profound that in the United States today there is a national holiday dedicated to the enduring energy in Dr. King's life and message.

As a young pastor, his eloquent voice and strategic planning for the 1955 Montgomery bus boycott quickly pushed him into the top ranks of the U.S. civil rights movement. King developed a philosophy of nonviolent direct action through which oppressed people, especially blacks suffering in the 1950s under a system of legal segregation in the southern U.S., could courageously challenge the people, the attitudes and the legal structures that oppressed them. Today, his principles and the courage of those who followed his teachings is enshrined as a core chapter in what Americans teach their children.

Although celebrated now, this path was never easy for King. He was jailed along the way and eventually was assassinated at the age of 39.

At the core of King's movement was his organization of the Southern Christian Leadership Conference, which helped to coordinate local struggles from Selma to Memphis as well as national campaigns for civil rights legislation in Congress. As president of the SCLC, King also appealed directly to the nation's conscience through marches and speeches.

In his years of activism, King boldly tackled "the giant triplets of racism, materialism and militarism," becoming a prophet and activist who was recognized for his impact with the Nobel Peace Prize in 1964, the youngest person to receive this global honor.

King's philosophy of nonviolence derived from Jesus' teaching in the Sermon on the Mount (Matthew 5-7), but it was from the Hindu activist Mahatma Gandhi that King drew the methodology for putting Jesus' teachings into practice in the segregationist South. As he wrote: "Christ furnished the spirit and motivation, while Gandhi furnished the method." In 1959 he traveled to India and deepened his understanding of nonviolence in dialogue with the Gandhi family and others active in the movement.

Many Jewish leaders joined in the struggle for civil rights for black citizens – and many Jewish activists were brutalized while working shoulder to shoulder with non-Jews in King's movement. Together, these people found new ways to pray and work together for change.

King was a consistent prophetic voice against anti-Semitism as expressed by both segregationists and by some within his own black community. King said, "I solemnly pledge to do my utmost to uphold the fair name of the Jews – because bigotry in any form is an affront to us all." He was an early advocate for the freedom of Jews who also were facing fierce discrimination in the Soviet Union.

In *Where Do We Go From Here: Chaos or Community?* King wrote, "When I speak of love, I am speaking of that force which all the great religions have seen as the supreme unifying principle of life. Love is the key that unlocks the door which leads to ultimate reality. This Hindu-Moslem-Christian-Jewish-Buddhist belief about ultimate reality is beautifully summed up in the First Epistle of Saint John: 'Let us love one another; for love is of God, and everyone that loves is born of God, and knows God.'"

King envisioned a "beloved community" where all people were welcomed and treated with dignity.

For King, religion was not a cause of division but an avenue to the deeper unity of love that should be expressed in justice for all.

Questions for Reflection

* *We all know at least a few famous phrases voiced or written by King. His prophetic poetry has become part of the fabric of American life. What do you recall? Tell friends and ask what they recall.*

* *King died in 1968, but many Americans recall seeing him in person. If you're one of those fortunate Americans, what do you recall? These are important memories. Share them with someone else. Or if you don't remember Dr. King ask an older person in you community with such memories to share them with you personally or with your group.*

* *But, do we clearly hear the message of this national hero who we honor each January? Are we still willing to dream risky dreams with King?*

* *Is our faith an isolated part of our personal reflections – or does it move us to connect with other people and the powerful spiritual principles of love and justice that King proclaimed?*

• *What programs have you heard about in your area that invite people from different faiths to work together toward justice for everyone? At the end of this book, we've got examples of such groups that you can explore. There's also an online home, which will be live in January 2008, where you can share ideas and learn about public events at <u>www.InterfaithHeroes.info.</u> Set a goal of simply attending one event and finding out about one local group to meet and join with contemporary interfaith hereoes.*

chapter twenty-two

Fritz Eichenberg (1901-1990)

Fritz Eichenberg was born in 1901 in Germany to an assimilated, non-religious Jewish family. He studied art and became a wood engraver. Then, he used his art to highlight his moral and social convictions, including his strong opposition to the rise of the Nazi movement that he expressed in a series of anti-Hitler cartoons.

When the Nazis came to power, Eichenberg moved to the United States. The tragic death of his wife spurred a religious quest that culminated in his conversion to Quakerism. He was attracted to the simplicity and stillness of the Quakers as well as their vision of a "Peaceable Kingdom" and as George Fox said, "That there is that of God in everyone."

In 1949 Eichenberg met the Catholic pacifist Dorothy Day and became involved with the Catholic Worker movement, which organized poor people into communities of faith that were committed to working together on social justice.

Eventually, his engravings became a regular feature in the Catholic Worker newspaper. Eichenberg's powerful and evocative images portrayed Christ in the context of the human suffering of the poor. A famous example was his "Christ in the Breadlines," showing a raggedly dressed Jesus in line with the hungry waiting for a handout.

As an artist and a man of great faith, he envisioned God coming toward us in the needs of our poor neighbors.

His depictions of saints were especially beloved by many who followed his work. Eichenberg chose to carve portraits, not only those saints recognized by the Church such as St. Francis of Assisi, but of other people who struggled to follow God in their own ways. These saints were drawn from many different struggles, different races and different religions. Non-Christians such as Gandhi were honored among his saintly images.

Fritz Eichenberg died in 1990, leaving a rich legacy of masterpieces, some of which are on display in the Smithsonian's Museum of American Art.

Questions for Reflection

• *Where have you heard that phrase, "Peaceable Kingdom"? It pops up in many ways these days from retailing to movies and from spirituality to the fine arts. In what ways might that vision be attractive to you?*

• *What artists seem to invite you into a larger community? What artworks expand your imagination about faith and human relations?*

• *Whether you're a religious person or not, images of saints are very popular these days. Saints show up even in music CDs, TV series, greeting cards and comic books! Are there saints that inspire you? Have you ever found saints from religious traditions outside your own, as Eichenberg did?*

chapter twenty-three

Abraham Joshua Heschel (1907-1972)

Abraham Joshua Heschel was born in 1907 in Warsaw, Poland, a descendent of eminent rabbis on both his parents' sides of the family. He studied in Germany under some of the great rabbinical minds of the age and became a rabbi himself. As the Nazis came to power Heschel escaped first to England and then to the United States. He eventually became a professor at the Jewish Theological Seminary of America, the main seminary for Conservative Judaism.

Heschel sought to balance a serious concern for Jewish law as a traditional part of everyday Jewish life with a deeper love for the spirit of the law. He explored that delicate but important balance between faithful observance and legalism.

He especially studied the prophets and applied their teachings to the issues of social justice in the United States. At that time most Jewish theologians in the world of academia never ventured far from their classrooms. Few academics dove into the rising struggles over justice and civil rights.

Heschel blazed a courageous path. He taught that the prophetic tradition required him to engage in the U.S. civil rights movement as well as the struggle for freedom for Jews in the Soviet Union.

Through his involvement in social issues Heschel developed relationships with Christian leaders such as the Rev. Dr. Martin Luther King, Jr. He marched alongside Dr. King in Selma, Alabama, saying, "When I march in Selma, my feet are praying." He saw religious passions and commitments as a fundamental part of a healthy, faithful human life. No religion could claim all the truth, he said, since God transcended any particular theology, so religious communities need to be engaged with each other for the sake of their common humanity.

He raised these provocative and inspiring teachings, even though Heschel remained deeply committed to his Jewishness. In fact, he was almost Orthodox in his practice.

Throughout his life, he was committed to relationships with people in other faiths. Heschel was chosen to represent American Jews for constructive dialogue with the leadership of the Roman Catholic

Church during the Second Vatican Council in the 1960s, resulting in historic shifts in Catholic policy and liturgy that had been demeaning to Jews. His willingness to enter into these interfaith relationships also led to his appointment as the first Jew on the faculty of Union Theological Seminary, the premier Protestant seminary in the U.S.

Heschel was one of the founders of Clergy and Laity Concerned about Vietnam. He became co-chair of this inter-religious organization that sought to end that war, seeing what was happening as a challenge to the very soul of America. In his frequent comment, "Some are guilty, but all are responsible," he put forth the challenge to engage in the pressing issues of the day as a person of faith.

Questions for Reflection

- Heschel is one of the most-quoted religious leaders in American life, because he had a talent for expressing challenging ideas. What did he mean about his feet praying? Have you ever experienced anything like that?

- Do you agree that "some are guilty, but all are responsible" for many of the ills in our world today? What issues would you include on such a list?

- People from many faiths and cultural background speak out on issues of war and *poverty today. Can you think of someone who inspires you, but comes from a very different background?*

chapter twenty-four

Jacques Maritain
(1882-1973)

Jacques Maritain was the major Catholic philosopher of the 20th Century. He was born in a Protestant family, but as a student he was an agnostic. He later married Raissa Oumensoff, a Jewish émigré from Russia, and together they began an intense spiritual quest. Under the influence of the philosopher Henri Bergson and the novelist Leon Bloy they became Catholic Christians and entered fervently into the life and work of the church.

Maritain became a philosopher, developing a modern application of the scholasticism of Thomas Aquinas. He integrated faith, reason and culture, giving special attention to the relationship between individual rights and the common good. He initially was involved in a right-wing Catholic movement that eventually was condemned by the Vatican. This condemnation prodded him into a period of deep introspection and self-examination. Eventually, he became a vigorous proponent of democracy and "integral humanism" in which he applied Christian values of respect for humanity to the social and political contexts of his day.

A central issue for him became Christian anti-Semitism during the rise of Nazism and the course of World War II. Far more than a political challenge, Maritain saw Christian anti-Semitism as a theological crisis. He was horrified at the willing complicity of French Christians in rounding up French Jews to be sent to the Nazi concentration camps. When Germany invaded France, he and Raissa were in the U.S. where he was lecturing. Exiled throughout the war, he wrote fiercely and extensively about anti-Semitism, not just in its German-Nazi expression but in the ways it was expressed in Catholic settings around the world.

Maritain wrote, "It is impossible to compromise with anti-Semitism; it carries in itself, as in a living germ, all the spiritual evil of Nazism. Anti-Semitism is the moral Fifth Column in the Christian conscience."

He saw the suffering anti-Semitic Christians inflicted upon Jews as causing suffering for Christ as well, an attack on the very cross that was supposed to be a symbol of peace. He empathized with the theological questions Jews struggled with following the Holocaust and the establishment of the nation of Israel, but he saw his own mission primarily directed toward Christians. So, he continually called Christians "to purify themselves of those forms of thought and language which are warped by some anti-Semitic bias inherited from the errors of the past, and which have nothing to do with the essence of Christianity but prey upon it as parasites."

He wrote, "The only way open to us is to develop mutual friendship, esteem and comprehension between Jews and Christians."

Pope Paul VI honored Maritain, among others, at the close of the Second Vatican Council with a special address to leaders in "Thought and Science." In part, Paul VI, said, "We are the friends of your vocation as searchers, companions in your fatigues, admirers of your successes and, if necessary, consolers in your discouragement and your failures."

Questions for Reflection

- *Maritain wrote with strong spiritual passion. Can you share in this kind of passion for condemning anti-Semitism – and other forms of religiously rooted hatred?*

- *Where should this passion lead us today? What steps can you envision in your* community to help defend minorities who may be suffering from bigotry?

• When Paul VI said to Maritain that we should be, at times, "companions in your fatigues," what do you think he meant by that phrase? Sometimes we feel called to join the front lines of a cause, but what do you think about this call to share other people's "fatigues"?

chapter twenty-five

H. A. Mukti Ali (1923-2004)

Dr. H. A. Mukti Ali was the Minister of Religious Affairs in Indonesia from 1971 to 1978. His advanced education in Islam was earned in India and Canada, providing both Eastern and Western perspectives in his training. He developed a rigorous concern for academic research and brought that practice of research to Islamic studies in Indonesia, a mainly Muslim country. He was a pious Muslim who saw no contradiction between religious piety and serious research.

Mukti Ali believed that one's faith had to be worked out within the social context of a people. There was a dynamic interaction between dogma and practice, between ideas and society, he believed. At its best, this dynamic produced a living religion, and in Indonesia an expression of Islam that was integrated into the country's culture. As Mukti Ali liked to say, "I am an Indonesian Muslim," choosing not to split these two aspects of his identity.

However, not all Indonesians were Muslims. As the Minister of Religious Affairs, he launched government-sponsored, inter-religious dialogue, including many sessions in his own home. He also participated in global Christian-Muslim dialogs. One of his key concerns was that foreign aid and religious propagation not be mixed. He urged Christian relief agencies to give as freely to non-Christians as to Christians, especially since the former were the majority in many developing countries such as Indonesia. Sometimes, this attitude led to friction. Many Christian activists were not pleased by his viewpoint and regarded him as an opponent. Nevertheless, Mukti Ali did not turn his back on inter-religious dialogue, which he felt was essential in preventing conflict in Indonesia.

Development was a major concern for Mukti Ali. He saw the ultimate goal of development as "the development of the whole" person – and that all people should have this opportunity. This included both spiritual and material aspects of life. In the process of development, Mukti Ali prioritized social justice over economic growth, and he saw aspects in all religions that called for justice.

Mukti Ali's vision was that all people should be free to practice their religious rites and duties

– living in harmony with neighbors, even if those neighbors followed other religious disciplines.

He wrote, "The harmony of religious life can only be obtained if every religious group becomes open-hearted to one another." To make this work there must be an "agreement to disagree."

Reaching that point of harmony was a major challenge, Mukti Ali realized, so he encouraged people to try to understand differing faiths and cultures by learning about them from an inside perspective. To flesh out this dream, Mukti Ali organized meetings of religious leaders and camps where students of different religions could meet and interact. The dialogs and camps included Muslims, Catholics, Protestants, Hindus, Buddhists, Confucians and Javanese indigenous mystics. The participants formed relationships and sought common concerns.

Although his programs didn't achieve all he hoped, future generations of inter-faith leaders would build on his pioneering work.

Questions for Reflection

- *Have you ever attended a camp or retreat with people from a different faith tradition? If so, how did the experience affect you? If not, what kind of camp or retreat might interest you?*

- *Mukti Ali had a specific way of describing*

himself. How do you describe your faith, race and ethnicity to people who you meet? How do the words you choose to describe yourself express the priorities in your life?

• Mukti Ali used his own home to host these sometimes challenging dialogs with people from other traditions. Would you welcome a dialogue like this in your home? How would you plan for such an evening? Who would you invite?

chapter twenty-six

Imam Moussa Al-Sadr (1928-1978?)

Imam Moussa Al-Sadr was the leading Shiite Muslim figure in southern Lebanon during the 1960s and 1970s. He was especially concerned about eradicating poverty and stimulating education for those who were disenfranchised by the main social and political systems in Lebanon. He founded many social institutions, vocational schools, kindergartens, health clinics and literacy centers.

He also was a leading political activist. He founded the Movement of the Deprived to call for an end to Maronite Christian political domination and to protest government neglect of poor rural areas. When civil war broke out, he founded the Amal Movement as a military wing of the Movement of the Deprived.

In spite of his role in founding the Amal militia he was active in peacemaking efforts during the civil war. He personally led a fast for peace and a public demonstration to halt the siege of Ka' Village and Dayr al-Ahmar Village, two Christian communities. He made the Safa mosque a center for civil and religious leaders to raise their voices against the civil war, and he eventually left the Amal in protest as the violence increased.

Over many years, Imam Al-Sadr demonstrated a remarkable moderation and sensitivity to religious unity amid the explosive tensions within his country. He believed in a peaceful cooperation between faiths was a strong advocate for inclusion of the minority Shi'ia community in the politics of Lebanon. He participated in many Islamic-Christian dialogs and eventually joined with a Catholic archbishop to co-found an inter-faith social movement to help the poor and marginalized. He also organized a committee of Christian and Muslim spiritual leaders in southern Lebanon to work together on political and social causes shared by both groups.

Imam Al-Sadr did not stop at dialogue, and he wasn't satisfied to serve only as a figurehead in new groups. He took decisive and sometimes risky action. For example, when Muslim citizens in Tyre boycotted a local ice-cream shop simply because of the owner's religious affiliation, Imam Al-Sadr ended a Friday prayer service with a march to the ice-cream shop. People followed, not knowing what was to happen. When the imam arrived he ordered ice-cream. Then the marchers all ate ice-cream, and the religious boycott ended.

In August 1978 Imam Al-Sadr and two companions disappeared in Libya while on a journey to Middle East capitals in which he was seeking help to end Lebanon's civil war. They were never heard from again.

Questions for Reflection

- *The march to the ice-cream shop is a wonderful example of simple, direct, successful action on a local level. But are we even aware of public places in our own community where bigotry may exist? If you discovered such a place, what would you do?*

- *Are you comfortable with people speaking out on issues of war and peace in your house of worship?*

- *Imam Al-Sadr knew that education was essential for harmony among diverse religious groups. Are there any educational programs available near your home that teach about other religious traditions?*

chapter twenty-seven

Christian De Chergé
(1937-1996)

Christian de Chergé was a Catholic priest
who was the prior for a Trappist monastery
in Algeria. As a young man in 1958 he served in
the French army fighting Algerians in the war of
independence, a war noted for its brutality. During
an ambush, his life was saved by Mohamad, a
Muslim friend and police officer who shielded
him with his own body. They both survived only
to have Mohamad assassinated the next day. This
act of self-sacrifice prompted by the Muslim
policeman's faith led to de Chergé's conversion
from his secular life to Christianity. Many French
missionaries and religious fled Algeria following
independence in 1962. The Trappists remained to

offer a contemplative Christian presence for the healing of the country.

Following his studies in Rome to become a priest, de Chergé was assigned to the Our Lady of Atlas Monastery in Algeria. In addition to their monastic disciplines of prayer and work, the monks offered a place for Christians and Muslims to pray together. A building inside the monastery was offered for use as a mosque allowing chapel bells and the Muslim call to prayer to be mixed. He believed that we see the face of God in the face of the other person, and that specifically he had seen the face of Christ in his Muslim friends and neighbors.

In 1993 Algeria experienced a growing rebellion. Though most of the neighbors of the monastery viewed the Trappist monks as trusted men of God, some extremists considered them "foreign infidels." The rebels gave an ultimatum to all foreigners to leave the country, but the Trappists stayed, refusing military protection. Father de Chargé wrote, "For us it is a journey of faith into the future and of sharing the present with our neighbors, who have always been very closely bound to us." He sent a letter home to be opened in the event of his death.

In 1996 rebels invaded the monastery and seized Father de Chargé and six monks. Weeks later they were beheaded. De Chargé's family then opened and publicized his letter in which he prayed for forgiveness for his murderers with the hope that their action would not contribute to negative stereotypes about Islam or Algeria. He closed with a hope for heavenly reconciliation with the forgiven murderers: "May we be granted to meet each other again, happy 'good thieves,' in paradise, should it please God, the Father of both of us. Amen! In sh'Allah!"

Questions for Reflection

- Do you recognize the "good thieves" reference in the letter? Can you think of other examples from religious traditions of people forgiving others in such a dramatic, selfless way?

- Has anyone from another group ever surprised you by showing exceptional kindness? Have you ever felt moved to give such help yourself?

- There are many sounds that people associate with prayer. What calls to prayer will you hear as you travel through your day?

chapter twenty-eight

Satguru Sivaya Subramuniyaswami (1927-2001)

Satguru Sivaya Subramuniyaswami, known affectionately as Gurudeva, was one of the best-known teachers of Hinduism in the world for the last five decades of the 20th Century. He established an ashram in Hawaii that became the base for his global travels promoting the Saivite Hindu tradition. He taught a spiritual path of inner effort, yogic striving and personal transformation.

Gurudeva was especially concerned to reach the Hindu diaspora, so in his travels he supported the establishment of many temples for immigrant communities. He wrote more than 30 books and established the influential magazine Hinduism Today. The magazine alone was an innovative approach to interfaith relations, because Gurudeva shaped the magazine's content to provide well-written, colorful overviews of various Hindu beliefs and traditions so that non-Hindus would enjoy reading each issue. His leadership in teaching and media played a significant role in a late-20th-Century renaissance of Hinduism.

Though he labored to strengthen and expand the Hindu community, Gurudeva was also a leader in the global interfaith movement. He was the Hindu representative for the Global Forum of Spiritual and Parliamentary Leaders for Human Survival. He joined with other religious, scientific and political leaders to work together on proposals for what they described as a common human future. Such efforts were one way that he worked out his teaching that people should live every moment in harmony and love for all peoples. He was such a significant leader in this field that he was elected one of the three presidents at the centenary Parliament of the World's Religions in 1993.

Within his campaign to establish new Hindu temples, he welcomed the participation of people from other faiths. When he established the first Hindu temple in Alaska, he invited native people in the region to participate in the event.

People in the political community appreciated his involvement in peacemaking efforts in the wider human family, culminating in his receiving the

United Nations U Thant Peace Award in 2000.

With his death in 2001 he left a rich heritage for his monks and other followers to continue.

Questions for Reflection

- *Gurudeva used a colorful, well-written magazine to unite readers of many faiths in the enjoyable experience of leafing through each issue. What magazines do you enjoy that seem to welcome people from many religious backgrounds?*

- *Or, can you think of examples in which media try to divide people along religious lines? If this troubles you, can you think of a way to let the editors of such media know about your concerns?*

- *What houses of worship have opened in your region? Have you thought of visiting religious centers near your home to learn about how these neighbors worship?*

chapter twenty-nine

Th. Sumartana (d. 2002)

Th. Sumartana was an Indonesian Protestant Christian leader who first entered into interfaith dialogue over the issue of development. He was critical of using religion to serve narrowly defined viewpoints on development. Religious leaders must remain free to speak out on behalf of social justice, he argued.

In this mainly Muslim country, Sumartana entered into dialogue with other Christian and Muslim intellectuals to explore ways that their faiths could support people's hope for liberation from the poverty grinding down so many in Indonesia and other developing countries.

In 1991 Sumartana began the Institute for Inter-faith Dialogue in Indonesia, or Interfidei, the first interfaith organization in the country. Interfidei was supported by both Christian and Muslim intellectual activists. As Interfidei's director, Sumartana sought more than expressions of religious harmony. His broader goal was bring religious groups together in helping Indonesia develop a more open democracy.

He wanted Interfidei to become a model of pluralism. He wrote, "This pluralistic nature would in turn become the most human way to solve our social problems together peacefully."

This was a huge challenge and sometimes drew criticisms, but Sumartana was critical of the historical record within his own Christian religious tradition. He thought Christians needed to free themselves from their intolerance of Islam, if they were to become an effective force for democracy in this mainly Muslim country. He made the same point about Islam, underlining that Muslim exclusivity in Indonesia did not serve the larger goal of building a democracy with justice for all.

He liked to quote Hans Kung: "There is no peace within a community without inter-religious peace."

To support their vision of religious peace and democracy, Interfidei hosted seminars, conducted training in conflict resolution, published articles, conducted research and invited people of different faiths to share in common prayer.

In the late 1990s violence between religious communities erupted across Indonesia with many massacres and the burning of dozens of churches. Critical voices said that interfaith dialogue was ineffective.

However, Sumartana and others in Interfidei understood that the process of promoting pluralism and democracy was a long and difficult journey. Inter-religious violence should not cause people to give up on building relationships across religious divides but rather should inspire people to intensify those efforts, Sumartana believed. Ultimately, the relationships established through the interfaith dialogue by Interfidei and other interfaith groups were helpful in opening conversations that could prevent further outbreaks of violence.

Sumartana died in 2002, leaving an influential example for Indonesians as one of the nation's interfaith pioneers.

Questions for Reflection

- *Think about Hans Kung's comment that Sumartana repeated in Indonesia. What does this comment really mean? Do you think Kung was right?*

- *Should interfaith relationships focus on social justice? What issues do you think various religious groups could work on together?*

- *When you read news stories about religious violence, how does that affect your own approach to these issues? Do you want to shy away from such tragic situations? Are you motivated to act?*

chapter thirty

Harbhajan Singh Khalsa Yogiji (1929-2004)

Harbhajan Singh Puri was born in 1929 in the part of India that is today Pakistan and was still a teenager when he was called initially to serve as a heroic leader to his own people.

In 1947 during the violence associated with the partition of Pakistan from India, he was only 18 but managed to lead his village of 7,000 people 325 miles on foot to safety in New Delhi.

Later, he studied economics and entered government service. During his academic and professional career he taught yoga. In 1968 he left India, first for Canada and then settled in the United States where he became a citizen in 1976. He then changed his name legally to Harbhajan

Singh Khalsa Yogiji, known as Yogi Bhajan for short.

For centuries the followers of the Kundalini Yoga system followed a tradition of keeping their practice shrouded in secrecy. However, Yogi Bhajan broke with that tradition believing that the larger public could benefit from the practices of Kundalini Yoga. He called the life system "3HO" (healthy, happy, holy).

Under his guidance the 3HO Foundation established more than 300 centers in 35 countries. Besides teaching yoga philosophy and practice, 3HO promoted women's issues, human rights and education in alternative systems of medicine. He pioneered a drug rehabilitation program that was became highly respected in the U.S.

He also used his professional background in economics and his entrepreneurial skills to expand the health food business. Among the products he promoted was a breakfast food called Peace Cereal. He used these innovations to promote socially responsible business practices, such as a move toward using organic foods.

Yogi Bhajan was a strong advocate for world peace and religious unity. He met with religious leaders of all faiths, including the Dalai Lama, Pope Paul VI, Pope John Paul II and two Archbishops of Canterbury. He was a regular participant in interfaith activities such as the Parliament of the World's Religions and the World Fellowship of Religions, serving as co-president of the latter. He was an organizer of the "Meeting of the Ways" in San Francisco and was a co-founder of the Unity of Man Conference. The Peace Abby in Sherborn, Massachusetts, gave him their "Courage of Conscience Award" for his work on interfaith relationships and world peace.

In 1985 he established the first International Peace Prayer Day Celebration. The annual day of musical celebration and interfaith prayer has drawn many national and international leaders. Yogi Bhajan favorite saying was, "If you can't see God in all, you can't see God at all."

Questions for Reflection

- *Would you like to attend an event where you could see people from different faiths praying together – as Yogi Bhajan encouraged people to do? At the end of this book there are suggestions for finding such opportunities.*

- *How could your own daily diet build stronger bonds between communities?*

- *Do you agree with Yogi Bhajan's saying: "If you can't see God in all, you can't see God at all"? Can you think of similar statements from your own religious tradition? Talk with a friend about this idea.*

chapter thirty-one

Cardinal Aaron Jean-Marie Lustiger (1926-2007)

Aaron Lustiger was born in Paris in 1926 to Jewish parents who had emigrated from Poland. When World War II broke out, the family fled to Orléans. After reading the Christian Bible, the teenage Lustiger felt drawn to the Orléans Cathedral. He decided to convert to Catholicism, with the reluctant consent of his parents, adding Jean-Marie to his baptismal name.

Lustiger's mother Giselle returned to Paris to run the family shop. She was swept up in the Nazi arrests of Parisian Jews in 1942. Giselle Lustiger died in Auschwitz in 1943. Meanwhile Jean-Marie studied while hiding at seminary. He later rejoined his father and sister hiding in the south of France until the end of the war.

Lustiger became a priest after the war, which caused a complete rift with his father. He was ordained in 1954 and served as a chaplain to the Sorbonne and then as general chaplain to the universities of Paris. In 1969 he became a parish priest, achieving wide recognition as a preacher who spoke with sincerity, humor and a sharp intellect. He was appointed Bishop of Orléans and then Archbishop of Paris. In 1983 Pope John Paul II elevated him to the College of Cardinals. Generally considered a conservative—he called himself a "Modern Traditionalist"—Cardinal Lustiger maintained positive relationships even with people with whom he disagreed politically.

Criticism of his identity and his calling came from all directions. Some Jews, including the Chief (Azhkenazi) Rabbi in Israel accused him of betraying his people and religion by becoming a Christian, but French Jews defended him. Meanwhile, some French Catholics complained of his appointment because he was "not truly French," even though he was born in Paris.

Anti-Semitism and racism have been frequently and violently expressed in French society, and Cardinal Lustiger was a strong verbal opponent of such views. He spoke against xenophobic politicians, holding that all people are equal in dignity because all are created in God's image. He supported the rights of immigrant workers.

Twice he attended commemorations at

Auschwitz. At a mass in Lodz, Poland, for 200,000 Jews deported to the death camps he said, "The strength of evil can only be answered with an even greater strength of love." During a time of increasing anti-Semitism, Lustiger participated in France's Day of Remembrance of the deported and murdered Jews. As he joined in the reading of the names of the dead, he came to Giselle Lustiger and tearfully said, "My mama." The impact of his public witness was electric.

In 2003 when the wearing of Muslim head scarves prompted an attempt to disallow religious symbols in student's clothing, Lustinger urged the government to allow such symbols so as not to "disturb a fragile balance" between the state and religion.

Cardinal Lustiger was proud of being Jewish. He spoke Yiddish and entered the synagogue to recite Kaddish, the Jewish mourners' prayer, for his mother. He felt his role as a Christian priest was rooted in the Jewish vision of Israel being a light to the nations. He stimulated a French Catholic statement of repentance for the passivity of the Church during the Holocaust and collaborationist participation in the Vichy regime. He encouraged the development of deeper Jewish-Christian dialogue and was given an award for advancing Christian-Jewish relations by the Center for Christian-Jewish Understanding.

When he died in 2007 his funeral at Notre Dame Cathedral began with his cousin chanting

Kaddish.

Questions for Reflection

- Many people have multiple identities, if we think about this carefully. Some of our identities represent roles we play in our families and communities. Some people are multi-racial or multi-ethnic. Many people have identified with more than one faith over the years. How many identities have you had in your own life? Ask friends to share such lists and talk about them.

- If your life has changed, like Cardinal Lustiger's life changed, do you maintain positive relationships in all of the communities you've known in the past, as the cardinal tried to do?

- As we conclude this journey through "Interfaith Heroes," who else inspires you in this way? Who should be honored in our next annual list of such heroes? Look at the end of this book and online, at www.InterfaithHeroes.info, for ways to nominate names for next year's list of honorees.

How To Use This Book

We hope you want to do more than read! This book – and the larger interfaith network behind this new national observance of Interfaith Heroes Month – are inviting your interaction.

We hope you will not be a passive reader, just absorbing information and storing it away deep in your brain. Rather, we hope you will find a way to use this book as an instrument of personal growth and a personal invitation to help build hopeful bridges of interfaith understanding. Whether you use the book as an individual, or in a congregational or educational setting, we hope your reading will spark further interest.

So dig in, interact with the stories, and connect to the people around you in a journey of discovery that can help all of us build more vibrant communities.

For Individual Use

After the story of each interfaith hero you will find "Questions for Reflection." You might want to get a notebook or journal to write your responses to these questions along with other thoughts that will arise. Imagine the person alive and sitting in your living room with you. What would you say? What questions would you ask? What advice would you seek? What challenges or words of encouragement do you want to raise? Write down whatever comes to mind. After a bit of time, a day or so, read what you have written and see what fresh insights emerge as you get some distance from those initial reflections.

We also invite you to share your thoughts with other people whose insights you will find online at www.InterfaithHoroes.info That's the home for this new national observance and for all the news about our ongoing project to identify heroes. Go online, read the reflections of others related to the various heroes, then share your own reflections, questions and experiences. You'll hear from people of a variety of faiths who are on this journey with us.

Here's yet another starting point: Do a simple personal inventory, listing all the people who you touch in one way or another in your life. Is there anyone of a different faith who you might approach for a conversation this month? Offer to go out for coffee, tea or lunch. Invite your friend to go online and read along with you. Or, if you prefer, simply wait until you meet to describe what you're reading. Share some of your reflections on the daily questions and ask your friend how he or she would answer. Most likely, you'll find similar concerns and hopes emerging in your conversation. You'll find differences, too. Explore those similarities and differences.

Whoever you are, remember that there's a gift in sharing your experience. Your friend will be giving you a gift as well – simply in agreeing to share with you. Two good watchwords for your conversation are: curiosity and respect.

For Group Use

Most congregations host and encourage study groups. Or, perhaps there's a discussion group at your local library, community center or school.

Interfaith Heroes was carefully designed with balanced diversity so that groups across the U.S. will feel comfortable sharing its chapters. If your group is formed of people from the same religious faith, you could take the project a step further by seeking out a group in another faith tradition to join you for a study of *Interfaith Heroes*. Such a group might be found by contacting a local house of worship from another religion.

To make it an easy and comfortable experience for people, invite them to commit to specific dates, so you can begin and end your journey together. Later, if participants want to continue by discussing another book, engaging in further discussion or undertaking a common project, they can negotiate a new agreement that respects those who want to continue and those who need to opt out.

If you're looking for additional books for group discussions, visit www.ReadTheSpirit.com, an online hub that points readers toward such resources. It's the Web site that is co-sponsoring www.InterfaithHeroes.info

As your group gathers, you can select a certain number of interfaith heroes to study.

The group could take the heroes in the order they appear in the book, or the heroes could be studied by grouping them in various historical periods such as early role models (Negus, Maimonides, Francis and Al-Kamil, Rumi, Akbar and Mendelssohn), India's struggle against the British Empire (Tagore, Gandhi, Ghaffar Khan, Lester), the Holocaust (Hillesum, Albanian Muslims, Buber, Trocmé, Maritan), U.S. human rights (Williams, the Grimké sisters, Thurman, King, Heschel), global rights (Montefiore, Buber, Ali, al-Sadr, Sumartana, Lustiger) and labors of love (Szold, del Vasto, Eichenberg, de Chergé, Subramuniyaswami, Khalsa).

Group participants could be assigned the readings before coming to the group sessions, at which time the group would discuss the questions for reflection about each one. The discussions could overlap from one hero's work and witness to another, because many of the heroes we are honoring dealt with similar challenges and themes.

In the discussions, invite group members to apply the insights gained from these heroes to our own contemporary issues, challenges and opportunities.

One way to ensure a higher degree of participation is to invite volunteers from the group to share in leading the discussion each week. If three, four or five group members each agree to present one story for discussion, the investment in the group is shared and the work load for leading the group does not become a burden on a single person. Each presenter could be asked to make an initial personal reflection or response to launch the group discussion. The presenter could also go to our online materials to gather additional reflections on the various heroes, sharing particularly pertinent comments with the group to stimulate further discussion.

For School Use

Here's the big question in public schools any time the concept of "faith" is raised: What is permitted under the U.S. Constitution? Clearly, public-school educators cannot promote religion or lead their students in religious experiences – but educators in the social sciences, history and humanities know that religion is a matter of social, historical and cultural significance. Teaching about the impact of religion in these subject areas is a standard part of the curriculum in many school systems, especially at the high school level.

It's not only permitted, but many school districts now are developing innovative programs to celebrate diversity and teach students about strategies for building stronger, more peaceful communities.

Interfaith Heroes Month is designed to focus on these pressing issues. We explore the social, historical and cultural impact of men and women from a diverse array of backgrounds.

As students study these heroes they could be assigned to explore contemporary issues of religious inter-relationships, including contemporary political and social conflicts. They could discuss and write about how the examples of these historical figures might present constructive alternatives to religiously fueled conflicts around the world today.

In addition, many religious groups and congregations sponsor religious schools. The *Interfaith Heroes* book is an excellent resource for classes on religious history, ethics, morality or contemporary issues. To enrich the class experience, a school could partner with one or more schools from different religious traditions. Students could interact directly or online with students from other faiths to expand the horizon of their discussions.

If you are interested in developing such an online student-to-student program through your school, please tell us about it through the www.InterfaithHeroes.info site. We would love to share your ideas with other teachers.

Plus, we hope that individuals, teachers and group leaders will nominate heroes for our January 2009 and future observances. You'll find information on sending us your nominations at our online home. This could be a major source of energy and pride for your class if your nomination finds its way into a future celebration.

We hope that these 31 stories will serve as a

launching point for learning from others in your own community. The more that happens, the richer the experience will be.

So, read, reflect, then interact with others!

Further Steps on the Interfaith Journey

Getting Started

We live in a shrinking world with people of diverse cultures, histories and faiths. Merely getting along with each other is a challenge. In communities where hate crimes have targeted residents, tolerance is a major step forward.

But, many people want to experience far more than mere tolerance. Interfaith heroes challenge us to move even further. They challenge us to learn about people who are different from us – and even to learn *from* these "others." Think about how our heroes conducted themselves. Their lives are models. In their stories, we learn about making friends, laboring side by side, building things together, taking risks and working toward more peaceful communities. How can we follow where they are leading?

Almost every major metropolitan area in the United States has some form of interfaith or inter-religious network. Look up that network, perhaps through the regional umbrella organization for your religion. Whatever your faith or denomination, you'll usually find someone in regional leadership who is connected to interfaith organizations. When you've found a group you'd like to explore, call or email to express interest in local events and programs. There is no substitute for making a personal connection.

If you cannot find such a group, then begin with one-to-one steps. Set up an appointment with someone from a local house of worship of a different faith. Meet to share your concern about building interfaith partnerships. Maybe you can convene a small gathering of people from the two congregations to discuss building relationships. Perhaps you'll begin by sharing a service project.

Every movement starts with someone who has a vision and then shares that vision with others. When a group grows around that vision, people within the group will further refine and add substance to that vision. Eventually, a community forms. So, if you can't find someone already pursuing interfaith relationships, then start talking about the idea yourself!

In Detroit, our Interfaith Partners started from a gathering of Christian, Muslim and Jewish leaders convened the day after the terrorist attacks of September 11, 2001. A Muslim businessman, Victor Begg, called on people who wanted to do more than "praying and holding hands" to form a new, more-active organization. We began dreaming together. Then, we broadened our circle of dreamers.

Sometimes, our discussions were difficult. We found huge barriers of mistrust and misunderstanding between us, but we kept working on our partnership. We discovered umbrella organizations in the Jewish, Muslim and Christian communities that connected to many congregations and other groups: The Council of Islamic Organizations of Michigan, the Jewish Community Council and the Metropolitan Christian Council. We discovered an organization already working with members from different faiths, the National Conference for Community and Justice, which is now known as the Michigan Roundtable for Diversity and Inclusion. We discovered other interfaith networks, such as the World Sabbath and Wings for Peace. We also found local clergy associations that had crossed traditional boundaries of faith.

Discovering people who already were working on similar dreams quickly enlarged our network. We developed some new programs as Interfaith Partners, but a major part of work became coordinating these existing programs – linking individual ideas into larger dreams we all can share.

Program Ideas

Gather a few interested people and you will discover that there is an enormous array of potential programs: Art exhibitions, blood drives, food drives, concerts, reading circles and interfaith worship are just some of the many events successfully developed by interfaith groups.

Christian, Muslim and Jewish groups have held "Abrahamic salons" to discuss books such as Bruce

Feiler's *Abraham: A Journey to the Heart of Three Faiths* or *The Faith Club: A Muslim, A Christian, A Jew—Three Women Search for Understanding* by Ranya Idliby, Suzanne Oliver, and Priscilla Warner. Bruce Feiler's website has information about how to start a salon: http://www.brucefeiler.com/discussions/start.html

Reuniting the Children of Abraham is another extraordinary initiative that emerged from the dialogue of Christian, Muslim and Jewish teens in the Detroit area. Together, they produced a play with the help of a professional dramatist and director. Currently, a multi-media toolkit developed through this project is available for other groups to explore. The first part of the toolkit is a Powerpoint presentation developed with University of Michigan scholars, outlining the shared historical roots of the three religions and how prejudice and stereotyping contribute to violence in our world. The second part is a documentary video, presented by a facilitator, which tells the inspiring story of how this interfaith group of teens came together, learned from each other and worked to produce a remarkable theatrical performance. The documentary is followed by dialogue with the audience. For more information about Reuniting the Children of Abraham, visit www.thechildrenofabrahamproject.org or contact Brenda Naomi Rosenberg at pathways2peace@comcast.net

Habitat Humanity also has developed interfaith projects, in this case, aimed at building homes for poor families. These hands-on projects generate a great deal of participation. There is nothing like working side-by-side to build relationships. Look for information at www.habitat.org/cr/interfaith.aspx

The Massachusetts Council of Churches has published helpful guidelines for interfaith events. Among other things, the guidelines can help you ensure that you won't insult neighbors through simple lack of knowledge. The guidelines are at www.masscouncilofchurches.org/docs/Brodeur%20article.htm

There are lots of resources to help you in your work.

So take the leap, find some friends, and begin sharing your dreams!

Sources

Here are some of the sources we consulted in preparing these biographical sketches.

Normally, this is the "boring part" of a book, right?

Not in this case! We are urging people to nominate 31 men and women who we will feature next year as the 2009 Interfaith Heroes. So, you'll need pointers to start digging for information on heroes. Perhaps you already have someone in mind. If so, we invite you, your congregation, group or class to dig into that hero's story and send a nomination to us through www.InterfaithHeroes. info

Jalaluddin Muhammad Akbar

Poems of Rumi: www.armory.com/~thrace/sufi/poems.html

Wikepedia Free Encyclopedia: http://en.wikipedia.org

Albanian Muslims During the Holocaust

Van Christo, "The Jews of Albania and their salvation during the Holocaust" www.frosina.org/articles

Kohen, Anna, "Remembering Albania's Protection of the Jews During the Holocaust"

Anti-Defamation League, Press Release: "ADL COMMEMORATES HOLOCAUST DAY AT CITY HALL; HONORS ALBANIAN RESCUER AND RECOGNIZES JEWISH SURVIVOR", May 2, 1997

Imam Moussa Al-Sadr

Imam al-Sadr Foundation: http://imamsadrfoundation.org.lb

Wikepedia Free Encyclopedia: http://en.wikipedia.org

Martin Buber

Ellsberg, Robert, *All Saints: Daily Reflections on Saints, Prophets, and Witnesses for Our Time*

Christian De Chergé

Ellsberg, Robert, *All Saints: Daily Reflections on Saints, Prophets, and Witnesses for Our Time*

"The Last Testament of Christian de Chergé, O.C.S.O." by Karl A. Plank, Davidson College, Davidson, North Carolina

Lanza Del Vasto

Ellsberg, Robert, *All Saints: Daily Reflections on Saints, Prophets, and Witnesses for Our Time*

Fritz Eichenberg

Ellsberg, Robert, *All Saints: Daily Reflections on Saints, Prophets, and Witnesses for Our Time*

Smithsonian Archives of American Art, "Oral History Interview with Fritz Eichenberg," December 3, 1964.

Francis of Assisi and Al-Malik Al-Kamil

Cahill, Thomas, "The Peaceful Crusader," The New York Times, December 25, 2006

Wikepedia Free Encyclopedia: http://en.wikipedia.org

Mohandas Mahatma Gandhi

Ellsberg, Robert, *All Saints: Daily Reflections on Saints, Prophets, and Witnesses for Our Time*

Sarah and Angelina Grimke

Lerner, Gerda, *The Grimke Sisters: Pioneers for Woman's Rights and Abolition*, Shokten Books, NY, 1967.

Wikepedia Free Encyclopedia: http://en.wikipedia.org

Abraham Joshua Heschel

Abraham Joshua Heschel: Our Generation's Teacher by Reuven Kimelman, The Association for Religion and Religious Life

Wikepedia Free Encyclopedia: http://en.wikipedia.org

Etty Hillesum

Ellsberg, Robert, *All Saints: Daily Reflections on Saints, Prophets, and Witnesses for Our Time*

Yogi Harbhajan Singh Khalsa

SikhNet.com: www.sikhnet.com/yogibhajan

Wikepedia Free Encyclopedia: http://en.wikipedia.org

Abdul Ghaffar Khan

Easwaran, Eknath, *A Man to Match His Mountains: Badshah Khan, Nonviolent Soldier of Islam* (Nilgiri Press, Peteluma, California, 1984)

Martin Luther King, Jr.

Ellsberg, Robert, *All Saints: Daily Reflections on Saints, Prophets, and Witnesses for Our Time*

Dekar, Paul, *For the Healing of the Nations: Baptist*

Peacemakers (Smyth & Helwys Publishing, Macon, Georgia, 1993)

Muriel Lester

Dekar, Paul, *For the Healing of the Nations: Baptist Peacemakers* (Smyth & Helwys Publishing, Macon, Georgia, 1993)

Aaron Jean-Marie Cardinal Lustiger

The Telegraph, July 8, 2007, "Cardinal Lustiger"

Sugden, Joanna, "Cardinal Lustiger in His Own Words," Times Online, August 7, 2007

Associated Press, "Cardinal Lustiger, Jew who converted to Catholicism, dies age 80", HAARETZ.com

Glatz, Carol, "French Cardinal Lustiger, Jewish-born promoter of dialogue, dies," Catholic News Service

Simon, Scott, Weekend Edition Saturday, NPR Radio, August 11, 2007

Wikepedia Free Encyclopedia: http://en.wikipedia.org

Moses Maimonides

Wikepedia Free Encyclopedia: http://en.wikipedia.org

Jewish Virtual Library: www.jewishvirtuallibrary.org

Jacques Maritain

Ellsberg, Robert, *All Saints: Daily Reflections on Saints, Prophets, and Witnesses for Our Time*

Jewish Reader, "When Judaism and Christianity Meet"

Wikepedia Free Encyclopedia: http://en.wikipedia.org

Moses Mendelssohn

Wikepedia Free Encyclopedia: http://en.wikipedia.org

Jewish Virtual Library: www.jewishvirtuallibrary.org

Moses Montefiore

The Jewish Magazine, July, 2004

Green, Abigail, "Rethinking Sir Moses Montefiore: Religion, Nationhood, and International Philanthropy in the Nineteenth Century," American Historical Review, June, 2005

Wikepedia Free Encyclopedia: http://en.wikipedia.org

Mukti Ali

Hadi Nahrowl, Angus, "Religious Pluralism in Indonesia: Helpful and Hindering Aspects" Inter-religious Dialogue, dissertation at: http://igitur-archive.library.uu.nl/dissertations/2006-0915-201013/c6.pdf.

Wikepedia Free Encyclopedia: http://en.wikipedia.org

King Negus Ashama ibn Abjar of Abyssinia

Wikepedia Free Encyclopedia: http://en.wikipedia.org

Jalal Ad-Din Muhammad Rumi

Wikepedia Free Encyclopedia: http://en.wikipedia.org

The Rumi Network: http://www.rumi.net/rumi_by_shiva.htm

Th. Sumartana

Hadi Nahrowl, Angus, "Religious Pluralism in Indonesia: Helpful and Hindering Aspects" Inter-religious

Dialogue, dissertation at: http://igitur-archive.library.uu.nl/dissertations/2006-0915-201013/c6.pdf.

Henrietta Szold

Jewish Virtual Library: www.jewishvirtuallibrary.org

Wikepedia Free Encyclopedia: http://en.wikipedia.org

Rabindranath Tagore

Wikepedia Free Encyclopedia: http://en.wikipedia.org

www.Nobelprize.org

School of Wisdom: www.schoolofwisdom.com

Howard Thurman

Thurman, Howard. *With Head and Heart: The Autobiography of Howard Thurman*

Burden, Jean "Howard Thurman," Atlantic Monthly, 1953, from Chicken Bones: A Journal for Literary & Artistic African-American Themes, www.nathanielturner.com

André Trocmé

Ellsberg, Robert, *All Saints: Daily Reflections on Saints, Prophets, and Witnesses for Our Time*

Roger Williams

Ellsberg, Robert, *All Saints: Daily Reflections on Saints, Prophets, and Witnesses for Our Time*

Dekar, Paul, *For the Healing of the Nations: Baptist Peacemakers* (Smyth & Helwys Publishing, Macon, Georgia, 1993)

Community Resources

Interfaith Heroes Month springs from Michigan's rich experience of religious diversity – and decades of work by dedicated men and women building programs to link our many individual ethnic, cultural, racial and religious communities into one larger community.

We know that many of our readers in this 1st Annual observance are in other states – and even in other countries around the world. We offer the following list for our many readers in Michigan, but also as a rich sampling of how one corner of the world has blossomed with a broad array of programs.

What's especially impressive is that this is just a sampling of the many wonderful non-profit and educational programs working in this area.

Take a look —

ACCESS
   Arab Community Center for Economic and
   Social Services
   2651 Saulino Ct.
   Dearborn, MI 48120
   Phone: 313-842-7010
   Fax: 313-842-5150

ACLU Racial Justice Project
  60 W. Hancock
  Detroit, MI
  313-578-6800
  http://aclumich.org

Affirmations
  290 W. 9 Mile Road
  Ferndale, Michigan 48220
  248-398-7105
  http://www.goaffirmations.org/site/PageServer
  "Affirmations is a 501 (c) 3 nonprofit organization serving people of all sexual orientations and gender identities."

American Jewish Committee
  6735 Telegraph Rd. Suite 320
  Bloomfield Hills, MI 48301
  Phone: 248-646-7686
  Fax: 248-646-7688
  Detroit@ajc.org
  http://www.ajc.org

Anti-Defamation League
  E-Mail: detroit@adl.org
  Phone: 248-353-7553
  Fax: 248-353-1264
  http://www.adl.org/regional/detroit/default.asp

Arab Detroit
  877-272-2944
  www.arabdetroit.com

Arab American National Museum
13624 Michigan Ave
Dearborn, MI 48126
313-582-2266
www.arabamericanmuseum.org

Association of Chinese Americans Detroit Chapter
420 Peterboro
Detroit, MI 48201
313-831-1790
http://www.acadetroit.org/main.php?p=home

Bharatiya Temple in Troy
6850 Adams Roa
Troy, Michigan 48098
Phone: 248-879-2552
Email: bharatiyatempletroy@bharatiya-temple.
org

Black Bottom Collective (working with youth,
impact of hip hop on culture)
313-377-2048
http://profile.myspace.com/
index.cfm?fuseaction=user.
viewprofile&friendID=13367437

Chaldean Federation of America
30777 Northwestern Hwy., Ste. 300
Farmington Hills, MI 48334
Phone: 248-851-3023
Fax: 248-851-9551
E-mail: info@chaldeanfederation.org
http://www.chaldeanfederation.org/

Charles H. Wright Museum of African American
 History
 315 East Warren
 Detroit, MI
 313-494-5800
 http://www.maah-detroit.org

Freedom House
 2630 W. Lafayette
 Detroit, MI 48216-2019
 313-964-4320
 Email: freedomhousemi@sbcglobal.net
 http://www.freedomhousedetroit.org/
 "Freedom House, a non-profit, nonpartisan organization,
 is a clear voice for democracy and freedom around the
 world. Through a vast array of international programs and
 publications, Freedom House is working to advance the
 remarkable worldwide expansion of political and economic
 freedom."

Holocaust Memorial Center
 28123 Orchard Lake Road,
 Farmington Hills, MI 48334
 248-553-2400
 248-553-2433 FAX
 248-553-2834 Library
 http://www.holocaustcenter.org/index.php

Jewish Community Relations Council
6735 Telegraph Road – Suite 205
Bloomfield Hills, MI 48301
248-642-5393
General e-mail: office@detroitjcrc.org
http://www.jewishcommunitycouncil.org/
about/contact.php

La Sed
Latin Americans for Social and Economic
Development
7150 West Vernor
Detroit, MI 48209
313-554-2025

Michigan Darfur Coalition
Email: info@michigandarfurcoalition.org
248-642-5393
http://www.MichiganDarfurCoalition.org

Michigan Roundtable for Diversity and Inclusion
525 New Center One
3031 W. Grand Boulevard
Detroit, MI 48202
Phone: 313-870-1500
Fax: 313-870-1501
http://www.MIRoundtable.org/

Muslim Unity Center
1830 West Square Lake Rd
Bloomfield Hills, Michigan 48302
Phone : 248-857-9200
Email: imam@MuslimUnityCenter.org
http://www.muslimunitycenter.org/

New Detroit, Inc.
> 3011 W. Grand Boulevard, Suite 1200
> Detroit, Michigan 48202
> 313-664-2071
> http://newdetroit.obscorp.com/obsportal/
> *"The Coalition focuses on areas that represent the greatest potential threat to the community's ability to achieve and maintain positive race relations. Four areas demand our attention: Youth Development, Race Relation and Cultural Collaboration, Economic Equity, Community Capacity Building."*

Oakland Mediation Center
> http://www.mediation-omc.org/
> 550 Hulet Drive, Suite 102
> Bloomfield Hills, MI 48302
> Tel. (248) 338-4280
> Fax. (248) 338-0480
> *"A non-profit, volunteer based organization established through the Community Dispute Resolution Program (CDRP) to offer mediation as an alternative to the traditional adversarial dispute resolution in the courts. We offer mediation, conciliation, facilitation and education services to Oakland County residents."*

Phillipine American Community Center
> 17356 NorthLand Park Court
> Southfield, Michigan 48075
> Telephone: (248) 443-7037
> http://www.paccm.org/contactus.html

Race Relations & Diversity Task Force,
  Birmingham Bloomfield Area
  The Community House
  380 Bates Street
  Birmingham, MI 48009
  Phone: 248-644-5832
  www.RaceRelationsDivesity.org
  "We come together to welcome diversity and to build and
  maintain an open community which will not tolerate racism
  or prejudice."

Starr Commonwealth Healing of Racism Institute
  13725 Starr Commonwealth Road
  Albion, MI 49224-9580
  (800) 315-8640
  http://www.starr.org/site/
  PageServer?pagename=ndk_training

Triangle Foundation
  Phone: 313-537-7000
  http://www.tri.org/
  "Michigan's leading organization serving the gay, lesbian,
  bisexual, transgender and allied communities."

United Way for Southeastern Michigan
  1212 Griswold
  Detroit
  313-226-9270
  uwsem.org

CPSIA information can be obtained
at www.ICGtesting.com
Printed in the USA
FFOW04n1704280316
22739FF